D0808024

BUBBLEGUM SUN

CLAUDETTE WALKER
&
MATRIX FILIA

Abacus Books, Inc.
P.O. Box 56450
St. Petersburg, Florida 33732-6450, U.S.A.
www.abacusbooks.com

First Edition

Library of Congress Cataloging in Publication Data
Walker, C., & Filia, M.
BUBBLEGUM SUN
I. Title

ISBN# 0-9716292-4-2
EAN# 978-0-9716292-4-0

Printed in the United States of America
Set in Times New Roman

Dedicated to Deborah Walker and the "feral" children coming of age in the 1960s...

CHAPTER ONE

Ultimately, above all else, our generation believed the songs were for us – a private serenade to our youth, but alas, we learned … the lyrics lied.

I hear Marvin Gaye's "A Change Is Gonna Come," playing on the radio from the back seat of an airport car. As it turns out, it's driven by Jay, an old family friend. Even though he tells me that the city is starting to come back, I see through the car windows an empty shell of the once booming metropolis of Detroit passing by. The cause of destruction wasn't the fires and violence of that summer now past, but disappearing jobs, time itself.

Each vignette is from a long-ago life, one engulfed in the times. It was a decade of "feral" youths coming of age in the '60s. Without regret, I'm going to take you back to the joy, laughter, the trials, and tribulations of a more innocent version of Claudette Sutton.

However, even then, I somehow knew the summer, that summer, would forever make its mark – the Bubblegum Sun would scorch the essence of our lives.

Together, suspended upon this "Pale Blue Dot" (with a tip of the hat to Carl Sagan), our feet are tenuously planted on these earthly sands – the sands of time. On that sand, our Beach, a microcosm of tiny glass particles, existed in the 1960s era. That decade, in a thousand small towns, will now and forever be compressed into the summer of 1967. Damn, that was a mouthful. Although I may sound dramatic, stay with me . . .

The last day of school isn't like any other; the possibilities are unlimited. My shoes had already left my feet and my toes were touching God's green earth. Somehow, the air seemed fresher – and I know the grass was surely greener than when I entered school that day. Was it the feel and the sweet scent of freedom? Liberty's sound was the ringing of that last bell, followed by the frantic dash of students escaping, all of them running everywhere and nowhere, just away.

We had two major public-school systems, the town and the Beach. There was a dividing line between the school districts; it was a main thoroughfare called "North Dixie Highway." Why did we call our neighborhood "The Beaches?" After all, the area is actually many communities positioned on Lake Erie. Man-made beaches existed for the residents. They were adjacent to a three-foot breakwall, built to protect villages of cottage-style houses. All this was engulfed by the glowing sunshine of the sky and in our lives.

They were our beach communities, butted up to the shore of beautiful Lake Erie. Yes, there was a time that the water sparkled in the sun's rays – water so clear that the sandy bottom was visible. Sadly, the area's industry would soon show its ugly side. Many years of factory runoff from paper mills, auto plants, and other industries would make the water odious. Thankfully, that period was followed by years of recovery. The lake would see the worst of its pollution and restoration long after I was gone, more than forty years now.

"Beach kids," as we were known, lived by a different set of rules – or to be honest, a lack of them. At fifteen, we were to be blessed or doomed, without really understanding that our freedom could lead to glory or hell in the days and decades to come.

Don't get me wrong, we understood our privilege, far more than the kids who lived in town. We simply didn't understand the price that some would pay. However, as we all know, when you're young you take almost everything for granted.

So, with our tastes abandoning the poodle skirts of the 1950s, we welcomed a new look – created by the Navy in the 1800s. The military's intent was to make sailors' pants easily removeable when wet. The use by those sailors of old was followed by Coco Chanel reviving that same style as "Beach Pajamas" in the 1920s. Her purpose was fashion for fashion's sake. Bell-bottom jeans had found a home with the 1960s generation. Our purpose for them was as a symbol of defiance.

No longer would women be trapped into submission by the skirts and girdles of the fifties. To the burn barrel with the cantilever brassiere, an abomination created by Howard Hughes, a fucking man! Let him wear it!

Everyone's wide-legged bell bottoms and the girls shedding of their bras signaled the rebelliousness of the new generation. Boys, looking to escape their fathers' decades of conformity, along with their factory-made

4

death sentences, welcomed these new girls with open eyes . . .

My community, give or take, was ten dirt and gravel roads that were perpendicular to the lake as well as two others, one near Dixie Highway and another close to the breakwall, that ran parallel to the beach. The "Woodfield, A Private Beach Community" sign at the entrance, meant just that. All entrances were fitted with large, heavy iron gates, surely provided by the local iron and steel mills. The coup de grâce was a manned private security guardhouse at the main entrance. All of this, designed to keep the world and police out, had some serious benefits for us kids.

The agreement with the county was that police could not enter unless called in by a resident – and who the hell would dare call the police, except for a murder? If we beach kids really did something bad, residents would just go talk to the offenders' parents. All the locals just wanted to be left alone with their families. They solved their own problems.

For years, that had worked just fine. A little slice of heaven, cut off from the world. Few would see the storms rolling down from Detroit, up from Toledo, and spreading not just across southeast Michigan, but throughout the country.

For us, the children of the 60s, it was a dose of paradise just twenty minutes south of Detroit. The cottage homes were not posh. But for what the neighborhood lacked, it provided more. There was even a ball park that had supplied privacy for legendary Babe Ruth to practice.

Swings, jungle gyms, maypoles, slides, and more covered the grass areas that led to the sand and water, again supplied by the local steel mills and iron factories. Less than three hundred people made up all of the families who lived in the beach communities.

So, it's safe to assume that about two hundred of them were kids starting their lives on those same streets, along the same beaches, all within a few miles, all easily accessible by the lake. These were the toys and playgrounds for a generation of children who had grown up together from bubblegum to rock and roll.

Between the breakwalls and the roads along the beachfront was an expanse of grass we called the "grassy knolls." Most of these communities had a large clubhouse set in the middle of their grassy knoll. All of that was really cool, but most important to me were the beach, the water, and freedom to roam. Now what was the word of choice that summer, cool or groovy? Anyway …

It was all connected, beach community to beach community by the sands of the glorious waterway; even at high tide, about four feet of sand separated the water from the breakwall. It was doable on foot, but was much groovier (picking this word this time), if you had a motorcycle and could drive on the sand. Oh yes, we did. I might not have mentioned, this Shangri-La also came with no age restrictions or license requirements for motorcycles and mini bikes.

I've no intention of performing a grand soliloquy about my parents. Simply said, they were cool. For us, our family life was one of love and childhood ease.

Here's a glimpse to set the stage for the trials and tribulations, freedom and glory of the '60s and our summer of '67 ….

The beach roads of private property came with a certain lawlessness. Ruby, my mom, grew up as a hard-raised southern girl. Like so many other women, she fled from the hardline religious, poverty-ridden hills of Appalachia as a young girl and found work wherever she could get any.

No matter what dead-end job she was toiling at, she started every day sitting on the steps of Detroit area factories, looking for a "good job in the North." At barely five feet tall, she would withstand layoffs, walk picket lines, and help to bring the UAW to what it would eventually become.

Mack, my dad, a towering six-foot-four, was a rough and tumble southern moonshiner in his youth. Despite his power, he missed serving in WWII because his eyesight was so bad that dark eyeglass frames with thick, heavy lenses adorned his face. He believed he had become fully tenured in a paper mill factory. As many would come to understand, with no real unions, the factories would close their doors just before workers' pensions had to be paid out, only to reopen under another name later. The companies got richer and the workers got screwed.

During their time together, my parents embraced their private life, as the last rebels of their generation. We should find no surprise in the fact they would raise their daughters to be independent, as rebels of their times.

Life had been anything but easy for my parents before marrying in the 1950s. We were what they call a second family. There were divorces and children much older. We never really knew most of our half-siblings well. Simply said, there was too much anger, blame, child support, alimony – really, most of the exact same problems we still see among blended families today.

Throughout my story you will read that many problems and issues don't really change with time. In these all-too-common situations, long ago and many mea culpas later, I stopped apologizing for getting my parents the second time around. I won in the luck of the draw.

Much of this happened during the many moons before my sister and I were born, in a time before life in the factories of Detroit, before their experience in the industrial north convinced them of a better life. The rural south and the Great Depression had deprived their stomachs and souls of so many important things. My sixteen-year-old sister Deb and I would have all of those things and even more from our folk's fat paychecks.

9

This was my parents' plan, pure and simple, "make a better life for our girls." For the most part it seemed to work; we wanted for nothing. Looking back and being a hard-working woman all my life, I now realize the sheer exhaustion they must have experienced.

Calls for school cupcakes for the bake sale or class parties were met with my mother saying, "Mack, call Liparoto's." Even then I think cupcakes were eight or ten dollars a dozen at the local bakery, but they cost less than she made in an hour of assembly line work at Ford Motor Company. By the way, Liparoto's was one of the best bakeries I've ever found.

My beautiful birthday doll cakes all came from there, and oh my god, the cinnamon bread! I've lived well and traveled far and wide – NYC, California, Florida, most states, and too many countries and islands to list. Let's just say no one really sees all the world, but I've seen my share. My time has even included living for an autumn of writing next door to a damn good bakery in the Pocono Mountains. You know, it was just a morning's backyard stumble away in a bathrobe… can't remember the name, but they were a close second to that wonderful beach bakery.

Some salty teachers and other mothers showed their irritation because Mom didn't bake the cupcakes. It would only take one person saying, "Don't you bake?" My mother would sound off like the west wind and she was funny, laughingly saying, "I make the money to buy the damn cupcakes!" Mom took no prisoners in life.

Dad was much more easygoing, with a real laissez-faire attitude with us girls. After all, who would dare say anything to the gentle creature, especially one with a history in our town of being one really bad boy before he married my mother. I bet you can guess who ruled the roost at our house – Ruby, my mom. My parents were truly an old-fashioned love story.

My sister Deb was quite smart. Her looks were also somewhere between real pretty and straight beautiful, with her porcelain skin, short blonde hair, well-developed body and long legs. However, that summer she had developed a sense of social consciousness and demonstrated her rebellion with her attire – all the way to the Angela Davis pin that adorned every shirt she wore. Despite that, she too was easygoing, with the clear "chill" attitude of the '60s gushing out her pores.

Our last school dance that year was themed "Psych-Out," a celebration of the psychedelic era. A female art teacher had Deb dressed in a leopard swim suit while the art class painted her body with glow in the dark paint. For weeks before the dance, they had recorded her on Super 8 video, lit by black lights, as she danced to music like Goldie Hawn on Laugh-In.

Before the opening of the dance, the doors stayed closed until all of the crowd arrived, so all of us went into the school gym at once. With the psychedelic lights pulsating and music already playing, we entered to giant videos of a dancing, glowing Deb displayed on every wall.

The contrast between us was dramatic, with me being dark-skinned and wearing long auburn braids that hid my pointed left ear. That earned me the cruel nickname "Spock" from the neighborhood boys. Really, I was a complete tomboy, at least on most days.

However, Deb decided to pick out my "Psych-Out" outfit for the dance. With my long hair down and flowing, I wore a doubled-breasted navy maxi coat, with silver sparkle platform heels. Underneath that long coat, for the "Psych-Out reveal," I was wearing a silver sequin micro mini dress.

Being a bit boy crazy, it was just fun to shock the boys at the school dance. But as they all knew too well – I wasn't ready to let any of them touch my body. To say I didn't have a lot of "going steady" in my life until then would be an understatement. However, I didn't care. After all, from the lips to the recently developed tits and curves … they were mine. Display it in wild dress, yes. Touch – no.

Now, I'm sure a high school art teacher would be under arrest for such a themed performance dance because it would be too risqué in today's uptight world. Although, who knows – the world might accept a high school dance theme predicated on murderous psychopaths instead. Strange but true! But really, the teacher was just ahead of her time with performance art. The theme was brilliant and using my beautiful sister, who was a great dancer, was perfect!

However, as much fun as we had together as sisters, sometimes Deb could be a pain in my ass. She loved to sleep late and I'd want her to go someplace with me. Waking a sleeping Deb was no easy feat!

One morning, filled with frustration, I slipped quietly into the room we shared and up to the bed in which Deb was sleeping. She was all cozy, covered up with a down-filled quilt. I placed a BB pistol at her covered butt and shot her in the ass, just to wake her. Calm down, there was no BB inside that gun, as best I remember. The pistol was only air cocked three times … for those not familiar, that's a bit of pressure – enough to sting, but not enough to do any harm.

She sprang up out of that warm bed like a damned jack-in-the-box and chased me down the staircase, out the front door, and down the road, with murder in her eyes the whole way. I was completely unharmed, simply because I could outrun her, but for me … grounded. That was my fate.

Being grounded usually lasted for a total of two weeks, however there was always the potential for a reprieve. Getting me grounded wasn't enough for Deb. She also served up her own revenge. She placed a pair of scissors on the nightstand between our twin beds as she said, "Sleep tight little sister with the long hair." I lived in terror of her and those scissors for two nights, knowing my dad was still hot under the collar with me over that BB gun.

14

Finally, I told Dad – and the heat instantly shifted to Deb, "Stop that right now! When you go for revenge, dig two graves, missy." She told me it was worth suffering Dad's wrath for the two days of revenge. However, we always forgave each other – and whenever push came to shove, we were loyal to the end, sisters in arms.

As we quickly fled the school grounds, freshly released for our summer's reprieve, my two best friends, Nancy, who you'll meet later, Matty, and I were all dressed in our finest "hippie" clothes. We had a plan – and that plan was strictly against my fathers' rules.

With our thumbs held out high in the air while standing on the side of Dixie Highway, we looked for a quick ride to cover the five-and-a-half miles from the Beaches to town. It was never very long before a car would stop and give us a lift. It was a much different, friendlier place and time.

On this day, a car full of older boys named Danny, Cory and Chuck picked us up. The boys were just cruising the surrounding area, having spent some time in Detroit. They told us they had just formed a new band called "Three Dog Night," and had come from Los

15

Angeles to visit Motown. Yes, indeed – the very same, very famous Three Dog Night.

Did I mention that our little world existed right outside of Detroit, and was scored by the sounds and lyrics of Motown music? Anyway, the guys were very nice. We thanked them for giving us a ride before setting off to spend the remaining part of our first day of summer's liberty in town.

We got out of the car in front of the record shop. This was usually our first stop for shopping. The smell of the vinyl records, the sight of the tiny, beautiful lady dressed to the nines who owned the shop, the feel of our fingers flicking through rows of album covers and the sound of the music playing – the store delighted every one of our senses. We admired and embraced the artwork that adorned every album cover that had been made especially for our generation. Naturally, we knew all of the music was for us . . .

Our real mission, of course, was to see what boys we could find to hang out with – and maybe smoke a little pot, if they had any. Days like this were many and the rides were plentiful for us. Almost always, someone we knew would give us a lift either to town or back toward the Beaches before we had to walk more than a block or two.

Although boy hunting with the girls was fun and all. I was eager to get home and ride my Honda 65, waiting impatiently for me in the garage. Dad had been buying both of us motorcycles for years; each year the new one was a little larger and more powerful. He had spent all of those years teaching us everything from riding to repairing. So, along with much more, we knew the average speed we could safely drive on different terrain to avoid dumping the bikes and ending up on our butts.

Dad bought us helmets to wear when we rode. However, because of his great concern that we would "forget" them, teaching us was everything to him. "In case of emergency, drop the bike by freeing your legs and don't worry about hurting the bike. Save yourself."

Drivers of cars in the beach knew that many of the kids were cruising around on these motorcycles and mini bikes, so they traveled at slow speeds. Nothing else would be tolerated. By then, most of us were damn good motorcycle drivers and reveled in the freedom those marvelous machines provided us. It was a false but beautiful freedom.

CHAPTER TWO

When it came to Dad's girls, Mom most often bent to his persuasion about our toys and freedom. Because Dad worked the swing shift, he and the sitters were our primary caretakers. In later years Mom would say, "We left the best one home with you girls. Your dad had the patience of a saint!"

A few days into our summer, you'd find many kids at the lake, floating on rafts they had made themselves or "borrowed" from some neighbor's house. The boys would push the girls off into the water. Our best retaliation would be to nab a small rowboat from some lake house and heading back to knock those boys off the raft with our oars. Then we'd quietly return the boat and hope its owners hadn't seen us or missed it while it was gone.

There were weeping willows near the lake, and their branches made great swings for arcing leaps into the water. When we tired of landing in water, we'd climb high into other weeping willow trees and then swing from their swaying limbs onto low-lying rooftops. Occasionally, someone would climb a pear tree to toss down freshly picked pears to eat, or to take a nap in the branches.

Sometimes, as many as twenty of us kids would play games of cat and mouse while chasing and sliding through the well-polished wood floors of the empty clubhouse. Often, we'd hang out the open second story windows. We believed we were invincible. However, that hot summer, the summer of '67, would challenge the very survival of many.

With our parents at work in the factories, our caregiver this season was the sister of a brother-in-law from Mom's first marriage. That's a mouthful. Jane was really wonderful. With her, our rules were just to "be in by dark," but she also had a forgiving nature when we failed to meet the deadline. Thank goodness, she wasn't one of those tattletale sitters. But she was going back to college and wouldn't be with us for the whole summer.

As I told you, I had two best friends. One, Matty Parker who lived in Lakewood, just one beach community over. However, she was from a divorced family and spent the summers with her father in the Upper Peninsula of

Michigan. When she returned, merely days before school would start again, we would hang out and regale each other with stories about our summer adventures.

Most all of the kids in the Beaches had known one another since we were toddlers or in elementary school. Families seem to move there and stay. So, we, the kids of the beach, had gone from cookies, hide-n-seek, water balloons, and tag to climbing trees, riding bicycles, swimming, rafting on the lake, and motorcycles, all of us together. And during that summer, our activities would expand to include sex, drugs, and violence.

I'm sure if you presented our information to a bean counter, the chances of our survival would have been twenty-five percent or less. However, we didn't even know what a bean counter was . . . and I'm sure not one of us would have cared.

Whatever might occur that summer, we never had any real fear of those kids whom we had known for all of our lives. Unfortunately, people and things imported from the outside world would bear much different fruit. Some of us would smell the fruit and know it was rotten, but others – not so much.

Anyway, with Matty gone, my first stop most summer mornings was to pick up my other best friend, Nancy Carmichael, who lived in Rockwood Beach, only two beach communities away. That is if she hadn't stayed the night with me. She did that a lot. Nancy was a vivacious girl and a loyal friend. She was pretty, with her blonde hair and curvy body already in full bloom.

With the sun shining brightly, the air slightly warm, and a mild breeze coming off the lake, I got on my motorcycle dressed in a bathing suit with shorts and slip-on tennis shoes. I was just ready to take off when I heard a loud noise, a pop. It filled the air and I turned with surprise. "What the hell was that?" I saw nothing but stillness and open road.

Peaches, my big black dog, jumped the fence at the sound and came running straight to me. Clearly, he'd heard the noise too. But with nothing to see, I told him, "Go home, I'm fine. Good boy!" Faithful Peaches ran and jumped back into the yard. Peaches was just like me, incredibly well-behaved. Not very often, but once in a while.

I'd shake off my startle that day and turn back around, only to hear voices from behind me. Gate Rouge, sixteen, a tall thin boy with sandy color hair, was always fast when he chased me. He was just one of our many neighbor kids. Overall, he was a sweet kid, just playing around.

Let me tell you, this beach was full of kids our age, mostly boys, but plenty of girls, too. Gate would call out while running after me on my motorcycle, "Claudette, let me drive!" Then Billy Jones would join in, "Give us a turn!" Billy was fifteen, and a nice, fun boy who never bothered me when he was alone. But clearly, he was a natural born follower in our small local bad boys' club. There are always followers and leaders.

I'd just rev the engine and take off fast, but being careful not to spin out on the dirt and gravel road. My goal was never to give the boys a reason to tease me by falling off my bike. Then I'd call out, "Catch me if you can!" In seconds, I'd leave the boys in the dust.

Far down the road and across a parallel road, there was a cut-through at the end of the grassy knoll adjacent to the hard sandy beach of the lake, right at the water's edge. From there, the sand and grass would carry me two beaches away.

Traveling on the hard sand of the beach slowed me down, but I always got where I wanted to go. Then I'd cut back off the shore and up another dirt road. A few houses later, I'd arrive at Nancy's. That summer, traveling on my motorcycle was great, because the Beach Association (including my dad) had agreed not to oil the roads. That was a huge blessing for me – a little dust was a whole lot better that constantly cleaning used motor oil off of my motorcycle and me.

Two things Dad told me when he gave me my motorcycle: "Don't let anyone else drive it," and "Never leave your beach." Well, I always stuck to the first rule – I figured at least that was something.

Nancy's house, was much larger than ours, but less well-kept, with a big yard lacking in grass. Most often when I arrived in front of the house, I'd see the remains of last night's adult party filling the yard.

It wouldn't even be noon, but men and women would be seated in lawn chairs, drinking beer around the fire barrel, nursing last night's hangover, or still on the drunk from the night before. Pam Carmichael, Nancy's mom, would be outside talking with people or they would be playing Simon Says games, with many of them still tipsy . . .

Mrs. Carmichael was real pretty, in her mid-thirties and married, but her husband was an enigma to me – it seemed like he was never around. I think theirs was probably a second family, too. Anyway, because of the drinking, Dad insisted that Nancy come to our beach and stay the night with me. I normally wasn't allowed to sleep over at Nancy's.

I think I only stayed the night at her house once and it was nice, uneventful. Pam went out of her way to give us some cereal for breakfast. She made me feel welcome, but she knew the why of my dad's rules. Anyway, Pam was a remarkably kind woman who loved her kids, worked hard to put food on the table for five of them, and often drank too much.

If the adults were outside, they would see me pull up and I wouldn't even turn the bike off. Pam's voice was high pitched as she greeted me with, "Hi, Claudette!" Then she'd scream toward the house, "Yo, Nan . . . Claudette's here." I'd quickly reply, "Hello Ms. Carmichael!" With a smile always on her face, Pam would ask her usual question, "How's Mack?" I'd tell her, "Dad's fine," and with an even broader smile she'd reply, "You give my love to him – and your mom too." I'd always nod and say, "Will do."

Pam would turn to the group around the fire, and always say something nice about my father. Something like this, "Boy, Ruby hit the jackpot when she married that man."

One summer day, while I was waiting for Nancy to come running and jump on the bike behind me, a man in a lawn chair waved, then turned back to the group, "Mack's a hell of a guy. Loves his wife and girls - that's for sure. You know he crawled under my house last winter and used a blow torch to unfreeze the water pipes for my wife while I was at work?" Pam quickly replied, "No surprise!"

I knew all about this because Dad thawed pipes under a number of houses every winter to help the neighbors. As a matter of fact, he lost a lot of folded money under one of the houses that year; it fell right out of his pocket. Early in the spring, Peaches found that money and brought it in his mouth, still folded, home to Dad. He was a damn good dog.

Usually, I didn't have to wait long until Nancy would come running out of the house and across the large front yard to me on my motorcycle. Almost always, she was carrying a blanket and beach bag, ready for a day of fun on the sand. That day, she was running a little behind and I had to wait a bit. She was moving slower than usual when she came out of the house, too.

It was just enough time for another man near the fire to stretch and say, "All I know is those young girls are real pretty . . ." Then he loudly called out to me, "Hey girl, come sit on my lap." Pam's face showed her rage. "Stop! Mack sees you doing that to Claudette, you're a dead man. Keep it up mister, and I'll be the one tellin' him!"

The man Dad had helped with the frozen pipes stood up tall, "You won't have to!" Then he punched the man that called out to me square in the face. He hit him so hard the asshole and his chair fell over, flat on the ground. No one got up to help the guy, and he just laid there.

I didn't even try to hide my grin. I would see this creep walking in the Beaches over the next days. He had one hell of a shiner; he stayed far away from me, never uttering a word. I'd say that was mission accomplished, thanks to the good guy with the hellaciously hard punch!

Anyway, as Nancy came out and jumped on the back of my bike, she called back to her mom, "I'm staying at Claudette's tonight." The embarrassment was obvious on Nancy's face. As soon as she was almost settled in behind me, she whispered, "Get the hell out of here." We took off together.

Latched on behind me, her arms squeezed tight around my waist, the wind was blowing through our hair as we headed straight for the beach. As soon as we arrived, we tossed the blanket out to rest on beneath the sun. This summer we did a whole lot of talking about boys we liked, the ones who were cute and who might ask us to go steady – girl talk.

For Nancy, there were only two boys. Her real crush was a boy from a "better family" – Gary Noble – real cute, smart and very sweet. For many years, his family had owned an established restaurant. He would remain just a good friend, but never a boyfriend, since his parents had plans for this boy.

Nancy's second-choice boy was no boy at all. He was Paul Lett, twenty-one, short with a cocky attitude. He wasn't even from the Beaches; he was a bad boy from town. The bright side to me was that he wasn't around much. The problem I saw with boys was that they all wanted sex. Nancy would say, "Not yet. How about you?" I'd smile and say, "Me – fuck any of them? No way!"

But I think she must have had sex with Paul. After all, why else would a twenty-one-year-old boy go steady with a fifteen-year-old girl? In the end, it didn't matter for long. Paul went to prison after he was involved in a shooting. Case closed – big romance over.

That summer was the first time Nancy brought a bottle of alcohol with her. Tucked inside her beach bag was a half-empty bottle of vodka she had taken from the party at her house the night before. When she showed it to me, she said, "They'll never miss it!"

I took a taste and spit it out. I'd tasted alcohol before; the boys always seemed to have something. I didn't like it as a kid – and that, my friends, has served me well in life. Today, I can have a social drink, if I want. Some who started drinking at that tender age become alcoholics, maybe due to their environment or genetics, it doesn't matter. It's sad but true, so now, they can't touch a drop. If they even have a sip of a social drink, they travel back into Dante's circles of hell.

Nancy, on the other hand, seemed to be thoroughly enjoying getting buzzed. We'd been friends since we were six, but there was something different about her that summer. There was something bad in the wind and it chilled me clear to the bone. Nancy's true personality had always been more than a little melancholy, with ups and downs.

But around other people, she appeared to switch on a bubbly persona that everyone liked. I could spot the change coming, because of a tic she had. Whether consciously or unconsciously, she'd push her hair behind both of her ears simultaneously. It was almost like it was a signal that it was time to put on her performance.

There she plopped down on the blanket, while taking large swigs from the vodka bottle. She didn't seem to mind at all that I wasn't partaking. Suddenly, with her voice trembled in anger, "I heard what that son of a bitch Steve said – I'm sure glad Tim punched him! Don't tell your dad, 'cause he won't let you come over."

I made that promise as she continued, "We'll drive by later and see if he's still there. I sure don't want him around my sisters. You know, I keep a knife under my pillow – you know that? No one's going to be fucking with me or my sisters!"

Nancy had four younger sisters and she would protect them. She was tough – far more aggressive than me. "Sure Nan, we'll make a few passes by the house. Are you still staying with me tonight?"

I passed her a cigarette, fresh from Dad's new Winston carton. Purloining the pack was my contribution to that day's outing, just one of the events of childhood. It wasn't long before Peaches came wandering up. "Look Nan, I told Peaches he was supposed to be at home." She smiled and we both moved over for him to join us on the blanket.

There we laid, smoking cigarettes and looking up at the sun filled sky above and the sparkling water in front of us. Nancy took a few more gulps before she broke the silence, "Should I write Paul back?" I looked over at her in a way that made it clear I really didn't like him. "No, you have plenty of other boys to pick from who aren't in prison."

Just on a little side note, Paul got out of prison at some time during a year that I was back living in town. I was driving my sky-blue Datsun 280z back then. Like all of the other cars I have owned, I worked hard for it – it was my absolute pride and joy.

It was late at night and I had just finished working a shift at my second job. I was exhausted, after working all evening until closing, tending bar at the high-end Colonial House Restaurant. That one-night-a-week gig was a way to supplement my income from working shifts and overtime on the assembly line at a Ford plant. I took that bartending job because it was the only way I could justify buying toys like a sports car.

I pulled to the curb and stopped my 280z in front of the bank shortly after two in the morning to deposit my paycheck in the night drop slot, before I went home to bed. I left my car running at the bank – after all, the night drop was just a few steps away so I would only be gone a moment. Paul slipped in the driver's seat and stole my car. Then he went around and around the block in it, taunting me. After a few passes I called out to him, "You're still probably on parole. One more time and I'll call the cops!" He surrendered my car.

So, back to that long-ago day on the beach with Nancy. She seemed to accept my opinion on Paul. I really don't know if she ever did write to him in prison, but she quickly replied, "No one interests me – well, other than Gary, and we both know that his family has plans for him that don't include a beach girl like me!"

I told her that wasn't true, but I knew it was. She was completely broken-hearted over this Gary. Nancy had fallen hard for him in elementary school and, back then, he liked her a lot, too. Over the years, his parents had made it perfectly obvious to him that she was just not the right kind of girl.

She had worked herself up into one of her tirades, "I'm gonna leave here. I mean it. I'm getting out! I just don't want to leave you." Having heard her express her desire to leave before, I asked, "Where do you think you'll go?" She told me, "Anywhere! You're going with me, right?"

I had no desire to leave, so my silence was my reply. I think it angered her, but she'd never stay mad at me for too long. I couldn't understand her attitude. Why on earth would we even consider abandoning this paradise? Some questions answer themselves, in time.

CHAPTER THREE

What is fifteen, but a miserable transition – no longer a kid and not an adult? That second part didn't really interest me, at least, not right then. Oh, I liked the boys because some were cute, fine and all. There were probably a few I would have liked to go steady with. Mainly, just because it was the cool thing to do. But other than a few boys trying to kiss me and run away or the ones who tried to look down my blouse, I had no experience. I just wasn't there with the heavy necking and the rest. I wasn't ready – or I simply hadn't run into mister right yet.

However, some girls thought the boys were the be-all and end-all. I wasn't opposed to thinking most days that they had "cooties," like the boys would say a few years before about us girls. Even then, I found the language that we used was interesting. Most of the terms had no value in the real world, nor could most of the words be found in my books. I couldn't figure out how they came to be used in the ways they were, but they sure could hurt.

Often, someone would say things to stop us from being friends with others, like, "Nikki Miller isn't allowed to play with us, 'cause she's Jewish. So don't go by her house." It seemed strange to me to ostracize her because of her religion, but I didn't know her well. Nikki was maybe a year younger. She and her family were always nice to me, although they weren't around much.

I don't know why, but I thought Nikki went to the private Saint Somebody-or-Other school. I remember thinking I'd need to put that on my "Ask Dad" list. I was sure if it had a saint in its name, it was a Catholic school. I also thought, "Why would she go to a Catholic school if she's Jewish?" Maybe she wasn't even Jewish, after all. Besides, who cares? Kids can be so cruel.

Ninety-nine percent of the time, you could ask Dad anything. He'd tell you what he knew and then say, "Now, if you find out different in those books, you let me know!" My father had a poor southern boy's third grade education. However, his father taught him by the age of seven that if you replaced the mule pulling the plow with your son, the mules lasted longer . . . Dad did everything in his power to see we, his children, wouldn't suffer the same kind of fate. He wasn't opposed to learning something new – or when he was wrong, learning what was right.

By the way, all the kids at the beach were White. I remember coming home and telling Dad we had our first Black kids in school and the other kids were really mean to them or just shunned them. He told me, "That's racist hate." He knew it all too well. The south he fled from was blanketed with that kind of thinking. "I'm ashamed to tell you how they treated Black people where I came from. Don't you be like other kids. You be friendly to those Black children – they'll need it."

Some thirty years later, while I was working a show at Cobo Arena, a Black man on a four-wheeler came up to the booth. He stopped, looked at me for a moment, and then asked, "Aren't you Claudette Sutton?" I smiled and replied, "Yes." The gentleman's face became as bright as could be, "I knew it! I just wanted to thank you for being nice to me and my sisters when we came to school." I suddenly remembered him, and his name tag made it clear, "Well, hello, Carl!" His remark was unexpected and he was so nice. We talked for a few minutes. After he left, I remember thinking how sad it was that he found my friendship so rare. But it was certainly most kind of him to stop by.

I was looking up at the sky that day on the blanket and quietly thinking, with my best friend and my dog at my side. My reverie didn't last very long at all before it was suddenly interrupted. A slightly drunk Nancy got up and announced she was leaving. I knew she meant going for a few hours, off on her own, to heaven knows where. But I also understood that she didn't mean that it was the day she would leave the beach forever, as she had always dreamed of doing.

She had become jittery, couldn't stay still, unsettled, far more than the growing pains we all felt. I think she started drinking heavy with that Paul guy, before he went to prison. What I didn't know that day would soon unfold before my eyes during the remainder of that long ago summer.

I quickly tried to regain her interest, just to keep her there with me. "Did I tell you? I heard a noise as I was leaving to pick you up, sounded like a gunshot." Nancy stopped, "Did you check it out?" "Yeah, but I couldn't see anything. Gate and Billy were chasing me, so I came to get you."

My ploy didn't work – she just didn't care enough to stay. By then, Nancy was standing at the edge of the blanket. She headed off, stumbling a bit while waving goodbye, then was out of sight in moments. It would be a lonely summer; I knew the writing was on the wall – or in the sand on which I, suddenly by myself, rested. I could see some kids not too far down the sand by the lake, but I wasn't really interested in hanging out.

It wasn't too bad on the blanket with Peaches, alone in my mind, choosing the things I wanted to think about. "In school, I'm bored and always thinking about something else. My Science and English classes are sometimes cool, but my books are usually better than the slow, slow talk and the squeak of chalk coming from the teacher at the board. Dad's after me, my grades are failing and so are Nancy's and Matty's.... He's really not happy about that. Now, I could tell him that's a direct result of me skipping school – a lot! No, I'm glad I didn't tell him that! It's better to just take the heat and make a promise to study a whole lot harder."

We had a girl, Missy Forgue, who lived at the very end of the next street over. Her house was right on the way to the school bus stop.

As luck would have it for the kids, the cottage where she lived sat back off the road and was shielded perfectly by massive trees. Even if a parent did pass by, they couldn't see anything.

So, what a surprise – that became our spot! Missy was an only child, kind of quiet, and never really fit into any of the groups. However, she lived alone with her mom, who left for work before school started and didn't return from work for a good hour after school was out. All of a sudden, Missy had friends! She had the skipping school party house.

Kids would hang out there, smoking cigarettes or pot if they had it, or drinking whatever alcohol they could score from their parents' homes. Maybe someone had a brother or friend over twenty-one who would buy for them. It all filled that house. I'd smoke pot and cigarettes and forgo the rest. We'd even bring our books to study, but, of course, we never got around to that!

A number of the kids had started taking hallucinogens that summer, like acid and mescaline. As I would soon discover, Nancy was popping those pills too. The parties at Missy's house continued after school let out for the summer, should anyone want to stop by. Although, in the summer I seemed to have other interests and really found it pretty boring at the party house. Some of the kids were diehard pot smokers, and with the new wave of acid and mescaline use, I skipped going by there to hang out more than a few times.

When I did stop by, it wasn't long before I realized Johnny was their source for nickel bags of pot. That was the going rate back then – five dollars for a quarter ounce. He also was the supplier of mescaline pills and LSD, both in pill form and as drops of liquid on paper called paper acid.

Johnny Gruise was ring leader of the local bad boys' club. He was seventeen and kind of cute. He was tall, with light skin, long black hair, and blue eyes. He was an early adopter of long hair, probably because he couldn't afford a haircut. His lifestyle as bad boy leader had made me anything but interested. Nope, not that boy, even if he was cute.

The kids all knew I always had money – an allowance plus pocket money from Dad. So, Johnny would try to get me to buy for the party. As soon as I'd walk inside, he'd say, "You're turn to buy for the party, Claudette!" Not being stupid or easily conned, I bought a nickel bag, said no a few times, and then completely stopped hanging out there shortly after school was out for the summer.

Oh yes, school . . . that topic brings me to my teachers. Teachers – now there's a subject this far-from-perfect student would like to touch on. I developed a love of learning on my own. Most, not all, of my teachers bored me.

That's the very first rule of anything that matters in life. There are not many absolutes. Thankfully, I did have some good teachers, including a social studies teacher who took the kids on an imaginary journey with him. Those were the type of teachers who would inspire my love of learning.

But the bad teachers were – well, bad. I found I despised even going to their classes. From their constant yelling over everything at everyone, to giving an order and then sitting at their desk silently glaring at the students for the entire class, they were awful. They waited for a pencil to drop and would start yelling again. It seemed some of them were always threatening or paddling some kid in the hall.

In hindsight, maybe my parents should have let me skip a grade early, back when the school authorities suggested it. Or, I'd have liked this idea, maybe self-taught at home – but not home schooled! I'd have liked the second possibility. No, on second thought, it had to happen the way it did. I have no regrets, for it all was part of the woman I would become. Change merely one thing in your background, for good or bad, and you may very well change the course of your entire life.

All too often, teachers would tell me about something for the third day in a row or assign a book I'd read the year before. And they would want a book report on the material I already knew by heart…easy, but too boring! I would want to talk to the teacher about something like *Dr. Zhivago*, a book I had just read. Where was this place in the book? Did it really happen? Whenever I did that, they'd say something like, "You'll learn that next year," or "That's not on your reading list." Out loud I'd say, "Yes, sir" or "Yes, ma'am," while thinking to myself, "I bet you've never read it, anyway!" As soon as I could, I'd look at the clock to see how much longer it would be until I was free of imprisonment.

In the summer, we had the bookmobile coming around and lending library books. Many summers before, Dad explained to them that I could pick any book I wanted, not just the ones in the kids' section. I discovered Aldous Huxley's *Brave New World* there and it fit under the seat of my motorcycle. I especially loved the pocket books, as I called them. They would fit anywhere, so I could take them everywhere with me. I was never alone if I had a book.

By the way, as of the end of that school year, my mother no longer had "most favored nation status," with the school, nor it with her. In one breath a guidance counselor ruined it when he suggested to my mother, "Maybe she should be medicated to calm her down – doesn't matter, she's pretty and will marry anyway. Maybe more homemaker classes?"

My mother told him, "Maybe you should kiss my royal ass!" Clearly, I could study and get good grades, but I was so busy thinking about so many other things. It wasn't my best plan, maybe not even a plan, but it was just me. Please note here, I have never needed medication to calm me down. I'm so grateful to have had a mother who stood up to the cultural pressure about drugging kids!

It was two weeks into the summer and Nancy had begun disappearing. I'd play with the other girls like Kim Swartz, fifteen and very depressive, who was overweight and seemed to always be eating. There was also Marlene Cox, fifteen, who acted like she was twenty. All the boys were really happy about that! They say Marlene had sex with a bunch of the boys. But then, boys lie and girls spread rumors. So, who knows?

I also spent some time with Alice Winn, who was fourteen; she was nice, stuttered a bit. There were plenty of other girls to hang out with like Jeanie, Tracey, Lois, Holly, Anne, and many more. Also, we had a small group of kids from outlying roads – the area that rested between the town and the Beaches.

A few of those kids were nice, but most weren't very friendly. The difference, in their eyes, might have been related to the size of their houses – their slightly larger homes versus our cottages, nothing more. Or maybe it was that their fathers were foremen and not factory line workers. It wasn't much of a distinction in the real world, but it seemed to make a difference to many of them.

I'd call them your standard wannabe prom queens. They were always switching one boyfriend for another boyfriend, always within their small group of friends. This I found a bit strange, but after all, these girls were on a mission; it was to "find a husband in high school," as the counselor told Mom.

Their only requirement was that the boy had to be on the football, track, or wrestling team. Really it wasn't unlike colleges in the 1960s, when girls were sent to schools like Barnard or Radcliffe to find future husbands at Columbia or Harvard. These girls were just fishing in a much smaller pond.

Most found their mates from the high school teams; a few got pregnant while they were still in school and others had kids straight out of high school. Many would live nice lives; some would suffer abuse and divorce. A few met the fate of some others in the drug culture. For some, it may have started with "Mommy's Little Helper," Valium. That's sad but true. For all their airs, the results for them were no different than the result of drugs on the lives of town or beach girls.

Few beach boys were like Tommy Johns, who was sixteen, real nice, very smart with great grades, and on the football team, too. Tommy really didn't like drugs being in the beach. Jim Clark, fifteen, was his sidekick in an anti-drug beach mini-gang. There was really little they could do or say that mattered to those selling the drugs, including Johnny. Most kids were cautious around Johnny, but Tommy and Jim were downright scared of him. They believed he saw them as a threat.

Years later and thousands of miles away, I heard Tommy was murdered at the lake. His homicide was never solved. I can't help but wonder if his stand against drugs in the Beaches put him on the wrong side of some drug dealer in later years. It broke my heart to hear that, because he was such a sweet boy.

Deb and I had no fear of Johnny yet. A few years earlier, the boys refused to let Deb and me play baseball and we didn't like softball. My father solved that problem. He bought us top-of-the-line hardball bats, balls, and mitts. The boys figured it out real fast. If we didn't get to play, no cool toys for the boys! So even Johnny didn't faze me.

Most often I'd just roam around on my motorcycle until I saw something interesting going on. Trust me, there was most always something going on in the Beaches. You'd find a group or two of kids hanging out on about every road.

CHAPTER FOUR

It was a Friday and I was just cruising around when I heard somebody calling me from a rooftop. I stopped, parked and moved close to the roofline to see what was happening. It was Kim, and she motioned me up a ladder. I asked, "What's up?"

She pointed toward the chimney and said, "Look!" I thought maybe a racoon had gotten trapped up there. As I approached, I heard Alice hollering, "I-I-I'm st-st-stuck!" I looked inside the chimney to see Alice in it. I called down, "Try to secure your feet, to make sure you don't go any deeper. I'll go for help. Kim will stay with you!"

I raced across the roof and down the ladder. Then I jumped back on my motorcycle and headed off to get a rope. I paused at every kid I passed on the road. Johnny, Billy, Gate, and Kara were all in my path, so I sent them to the house to help while I went to my garage.

By the time I returned, there were ten or eleven kids on the roof ready to assist us. We worked a rope around Alice and with all of us holding it tightly, Johnny led the teasing from the boys. However, it wasn't long until, pulling slowly, we had her out. Alice had a few scratches and she needed to come up with an excuse for her condition to give her parents, but she was okay. It was always good when we could do a rescue with no parents involved. Beach kids always did stick together like glue, especially when one was in danger.

I asked Alice how she got into that predicament. Stuttering, she said, "I-I-thought I-I c-could make it all the way d-down." I actually understood that reason, even though I had no intention of trying it. Like I said, we'd all climbed trees, swung from the old weeping willows, built our shack in the woods, played baseball, and more. Years before, the boys had gotten used to having to play with the girls, so it had become our normal. We were used to taking risks. Rescue needed? No problem!

A few days later, the first real darkness came over our Shangri-La. Johnny brandished a weapon. Even though the gun was only present for a moment and seemed to disappear completely, everyone was scared of him after that day. We all knew Johnny carried a seven-inch stiletto knife that shot open right out of the end. That was scary, but the gun was a whole different level. This was about the time that Johnny's and Billy's troubles started to escalate a lot.

They found a group of us hanging out and insisted we come with them; they wanted us to see something. When we arrived at an empty house, they already had the window open. We all climbed through the window, knowing damn good and well it was breaking and entering. Dumb old us, we did it anyway.

It was a summer cottage and empty this season except for a few old pieces of furniture. As I climbed back out of the window, I heard Johnny say, "We'll try another one." Billy was all for it, "Come on, guys!" I wasn't having any part of this, and most everybody else was hesitant. We knew those boys would steal anything not nailed down.

My family had to watch out for our two and a half car garage. My father and others built it on the back part of our property. It had an eight-foot pool table, box hocky, lots of tools, equipment, a go cart, motorcycles and our long forgotten three-speed bikes.

Because of all the locks, a long driveway entrance, fencing, Peaches, and the fact that the boys didn't want to piss off my dad, we were left out of their thieving, mostly. However, the few times we let the boys in the house for a party, one of my mother's rings disappeared and another time, some of my dad's coins went missing. We were sure it was Johnny and Billy, up to their old tricks.

The last party inside our house was in full swing with about fifteen kids. Of course, my parents didn't know about our parties and wouldn't have approved if they had – at least not without adult chaperones. Deb and I were in the kitchen cutting out holes in canned biscuits with a soda pop lid and deep frying the biscuits into donuts. One can had exploded when we opened it and we had just gotten the mess off the wall. In the living room, music had been blaring and Johnny was just changing the album. Kids were drinking beer and smoking. Suddenly, we heard a car enter the driveway and head toward the garage. Mother was home from work early!

We only had minutes – just the time it would take her to enter the garage, grab her purse and sweater from the car, lock the car, exit and lock the small garage door. She would then begin the 100-foot walk up the sidewalk from the garage and the house before she entered the back door through the utility room, then into the kitchen and from there, straight into the party room! Four minutes tops!

Deb turned off the hot grease on the stove and called out, "Clean up, Mom's home! Get out!" She raced to the living room and started pushing kids out the front door while hiding beer bottles. Linda grabbed the spray air freshener we always kept nearby to cover the pot odor. In minutes, the house was empty. Luckily, mom was tired and she told us she was going to bed and we should do the same.

Deb had her foot on a beer cap and moved it under the sofa, then we scooted up to the large attic bedroom we shared. Quietly Deb said, "No more damn parties! We'll sneak downstairs later and see if we missed anything or anyone!" I was surprised that Mom hadn't smelled anything in the house. Deb told me it took hours after leaving the factory before Mom's sinuses were clear.

We laughed. Deb and I spent a lot of time together at night, talking. If we wanted something from our parents, to sneak out, etc., this was the room where all our nefarious ideas took root, our conspiracies were plotted, and where they often were executed.

Deb was really smart and told me what was going on in the world. She knew all about the Vietnam War, the Civil Rights Movement, and the Women's Rights fight. Deb was also changing that summer – but I guess, thinking back, we all were.

Later that week, while riding around the roads, I heard the music of "The Doors" in the distance. Following the sound, I turned up a street. I saw a bunch of the kids hanging out at a house. It was on the far side of our Beach, and I didn't really travel over that way much. I stopped and, leaving my bike running, talked with a couple of people nearby. Eventually, I turned my bike off and walked inside to see what was going on. It seemed a few people in their mid-twenties to thirties rented the house. I'd never seen them before.

Johnny and Billy were flopped down in dirty old broken-down chairs. There wasn't much furniture at all in the place. Several older people that I didn't know were on the floor, surrounded by maybe five bricks of pot. Another brick of pot was open and spread out over newspapers.

There were pounds of golden pot, mixed with red and green iridescent pot buds. It was spread right out on the living room floor, along with a scale and baggies. A few bags of pills and some beers were on the table. Some white powder that could have been cocaine or heroin, I don't know which, was on a table in two small plastic bags. Next to it were a few small blocks of hash and a glass pipe. I sure knew what that was!

Today, I understand that heroin can be black, brown or white. Then, I was unsure exactly what was before my eyes, but it just looked like trouble. The older guys seemed to be working hard on packaging the pot, in between their gulps of beer.

Nancy had come in from the back of the house. Johnny passed her a joint, then she took a hit and passed it to me. I took a hit or two. Pot had been around the Beach for a few years, but I'd never seen such an amount! I wasn't a huge fan, but it was better than alcohol, by far.

Anyway, it was the social thing to do before I made a quick exit. Nancy walked out with me. Quietly she said, "Don't smoke here unless I hand it to you. They lace their pot with other drugs. This was safe, just strong, so you'll be fine." She turned to go back into the house as I was leaving.

As I approached my motorcycle parked at the end of the yard near the road, I knew I was really stoned. This was the strongest pot that I ever smoked with one exception, years later, at a party in Hollywood, California.

Now the "gentlemen" hosting the party that night, warned me to only take one hit and not too deep, because, "It's Thai stick." Of course, I didn't listen and was so stoned and paranoid on one hit I had to leave toot sweet!

Back to the drug house at the Beach. Because I was very stoned, I quickly decided to roll my motorcycle home, even though it was more than eight streets away. Gate, who was outside with some of the other kids, asked me, "What's wrong with your bike?" I thought fast and replied, "I'm just out of gas." They all laughed at me as I rolled the bike down the road. A few streets over, I sat under a tree for a while until I came down enough to drive it the rest of the way home.

Around that time, when I would ask Nancy where she was off to, she'd only tell me, "I'm just going." Sometimes it was an hour or a few hours, but other times, all night. I knew she hung out there sometimes, but was that where she went late at night, too?

Often in the early morning hours, like four o'clock, she'd sneak into our bedroom to pass out. Her most common method was by using the iron ladder that Dad had attached to our house. It was really a trellis covered in ivy and it was supposed to be used as a ladder for emergencies only. We girls had lots of emergencies! From time to time, she would also slip in through a door I had left unlocked.

Deb never told on her for creeping in or for me unlocking a door in case she needed a place for the night. Deb would just say, "At least she's safe." I think Deb knew more about what was going on, but she wouldn't tell me. Nancy was just there in the morning and my parents accepted it, often with a simple remark like, "You hungry, Nancy?" There was aways plenty of food to feed us all, and my parents never made her feel like she was a burden, whether it was buying her clothes, giving her money to go skating with us, or making sure she had something to eat.

CHAPTER FIVE

Our late mornings usually passed happily, and especially so on that particular day, with Dad's biscuits and gravy putting smiles on all our faces. Mom was preparing to go to work on the afternoon shift at Ford's, about forty miles away. After we all finished eating, Dad went outside as we three girls cleared the dishes from the table and washed them.

When we finished, I looked outside and saw Dad with Mr. Pines, a Black attorney, who was forty-five and thin. As usual, Mr. Pines was well-dressed; that day he wore slacks and a white shirt with the cuffs rolled up. The men were walking and talking outside at the green house across the street. I'd always call houses that Dad owned by color – pink, blue, green and so on. Dad had told us not to go over to the green house, but didn't say why. We found that unusual, but accepted it and obeyed him and stayed away from it.

Deb, Nancy and I were on the porch as Mom's carpool pulled up in front of the house.

She came out and gave us a kiss and a quick goodbye, "Love you, girls. Mind your dad." Purposefully, she walked to the back door of the waiting '66 Ford Galaxy. She was ready for another day on Ford's assembly line.

Mom opened the door to join Jay in the back seat. Jay was a nineteen-year-old boy who had just scored a job in the factory and became part of the car pool. A huge cloud of smoke billowed out of the car. She didn't mince words, "Damn you Jay, this car's full of pot smoke!" Jay was laughing hysterically as she told him, "Air out this damn car! Ford's assembly line may not survive! Henry Ford will be pissed if you're so damn stoned you stick your hand in a machine and shut the line down!" We could hear all of them laughing.

My mom's friend and co-worker Claire Grands, a very attractive Black woman in her thirties, was sitting in the driver's seat. She roared with laughter and then chirped in, "Ruby, that's Henry Ford, Junior, these days! Jay, step out and air this car. We've all had enough of your nonsense!"

Yes, that pot smoking teenager was the younger version of the very same Jay who just picked me up at the airport and is my driver today, more than forty years later. It took me a minute to recognize the now sixtyish man. But then, I guess we've all aged and changed. After all, getting older certainly does beat the other alternative!

Jay has taken me on a ride through the massively changed town with a fantastic play list on his iPhone. Then on to the cemetery to pay my respects to my parents, other family members, and way too many friends who have gone too early. I was stunned at the number of gravestones engraved with the names of lives cut short, many not even seeing twenty-one years on this earth.

This was our journey, before Jay brought me to the place that I still call home – the Beaches. I had decided to save the best for last. Yes, Jay let me know he hasn't changed all that much – he still is carrying a joint with him! Now, to get back to our story from days gone by …

Dad and Mr. Pines were standing in the lot next to the green house when the cloud of smoke rolled out of the car. Mr. Pines burst out laughing from across the street. He called out to my mom, "What's wrong, Ruby – don't you smoke hooch?" There were a whole lot of nicknames for marijuana then, like pot, weed, and hooch. My dad quickly jumped in with, "Got your snacks?" Also known as fine food for the munchies . . .

Mom was having no part of their humor, "You quit your taunting that boy! You two are just adding fuel to the damn fire!!" Dad quickly called out, "I love you baby; have a good day! I'll collect you tonight." The men started to head inside the green house. Mom called back to Dad, "I'll call you if I can pick up some more overtime."

Overtime – that was a magic word to both of our parents. Standard overtime pay was their regular hourly wage multiplied by one-and-a-half times or two times. Holiday pay was even better than that – up to three times their normal hourly wages. To my parents, that overtime was gold time. It meant there would be more to spend for "their girls." That extra income meant more money for college funds, vacations, weekend trips to Ceder Point, Greenfield Village, and Boblo Island amusement parks, as well as more clothes, better Christmases, and more toys.

Both of the men waved goodbye as the members of the carpool left for another day of work. It wasn't too long afterwards that Dad came home and told us that old man Wilson, who owned the green house, had passed away. He said he was buying it and told us not to be on the property. "I'll work there by myself until the deal is signed."

It was strange, since we'd usually help him pull up carpet, do some of the painting, or maybe just play in the houses while he was working. However, Deb, Nancy, and I really wanted to go to the lake that day, so we agreed. We raced into our house and put on swim suits, then headed straight for the water.

With the lake just at the end of our road, when we discovered the tide was out, we went home to get our digging gear. We knew from the level of the water that most of the sand bars were no more than ankle deep for the next few hours, so we walked with buckets, gathering clams. The water was warm and clear, with small waves splashing at our ankles. The sun was burning hot.

Nancy and I decided to go out a little farther in the water and sit on another deeper sand bar to dig. Deb, as usual, was calling out over and over, "Don't go out too far! The water will come rushing back!" Of course, we kept going. That was until we saw Dad in the distance, headed for the shoreline from home.

With buckets of clams, we raced to shore, lifting our knees high and splashing, just as Dad arrived. He looked in our buckets and gently put his arms around Deb and me.

Then he called out to Nancy, a few yards behind, "Come on, little one." She adored our father and ran to join us. Dad would often break out in song, and we'd all join in. Slowly, we walked the Beach roads together, singing and waving to neighbors we were passing on the way home.

Only a few days later, the malicious dog catcher snuck into our Beach again to try to catch Peaches. It seemed like he came around at least once every month. Good luck, Mr. Dogcatcher! Peaches was way too fast to be caught. I don't know why that mean old man even bothered trying; my dog was a mix of husky and wolf!

I might not have told you; Dad shared a farm with five other men. It was located a few miles from the Beaches. They had it just to grow food for their families. They all worked it in between their factory job shifts. Other than the farm producing plenty of food for the homes of all the men, one of Dad's friends bred dogs like Peaches there.

We also had twin Shetland ponies named Ike and Mike. They lived out on the farm, too. I think they belonged to all the kids of all the men who owned the farm. Maybe his share of the farm and all it produced was part of the reason that Dad never cared about us feeding most all of the neighbor kids.

It happened every year, and that summer was not any different. Right after the adults harvested the vegetables and fruit from the farm, a canning party began at our house. I suppose it wasn't really a party for the adults, but it was just another opportunity for us kids to have fun. Mom, Dad, Grandma, Deb, a whole bunch of the neighborhood kids, and I were all in attendance.

While the adults worked, we kids mixed work and play – actually, mostly play. When we were supposed to be gathering cucumbers for pickling, we began running in the back yard, throwing cukes at each other in what we dubbed, "The Great Pickle War." Once a playful sideways glance from over my dad's glasses happened, it was back to work for us.

Anyway, one day, I was seated on the front porch when I saw the dogcatcher trying to call Peaches on the road, a few houses down. Peaches turned and ran back into our open front yard, then jumped the fence into the back and hid behind the house.

The dog catcher approached our property and told me to keep that damn dog on a leash. I asked him, "What are you doing in the Beaches? Leave my dog alone!" This was exactly what Dad told me to tell him. I smiled and went on, "You see the dog? I'm gonna tell Daddy to file a complaint because you don't belong in the Beaches!"

My dad had a long-standing feud with that man over my dog. Besides, the catcher was not allowed inside our Beach. Remember, it was private property. "I know you park your truck outside the Beach gates and sneak in!"

That seemed to get rid of him as he turned and walked back up the road. Peaches was safe again. You know your dog protects you, so you gotta protect him! Just as the dogcatcher reached the next house up, he turned and called out, "I hear your father bought that house where the man shot himself. Must be an awful damn mess in there!"

62

I was taken by surprise, but I didn't let on. I called back, "So what?" like I already knew. I understood that he had just told me that to hurt my dad, figuring I didn't know. I thought, "I'll talk to Dad when he gets home. I knew that was a shot I heard, just a few weeks ago! It must have been old Mr. Wilson!"

Moving on, we had a bully or two roaming the Beaches. Mostly, our problems were with a couple of older jealous girls who seemed to appear in the area about two years before. They were worse than the few boys who were only slightly mean. The mean boys would pull my braids or steal something of mine, just to give it back later. I had grown up with them, so they weren't going to actually do me any harm.

But trust me, those mean girls were at least twice my size and threatened to beat me up regularly. Dad had already warned them that if they touched me or my motorcycle, he'd have them in jail. They were over eighteen, but still in high school – strange.

So, they left my bike alone, but not me. Usually, the threat was for the next day, just to terrorize me for a while. However, the day school ended that year, one was waiting by the door as I exited. Barbara Smitt flipped my braid in the air and said, "I'll cut them off the first day of school, next year."

Everybody knew she had flunked again and had to repeat her grade next year. That was no reason to blame me! Her threat was a terrible thought to live with all summer. I actually considered cutting my hair – that was certainly a choice, but I liked keeping it long. I just decided to wait until summer was over and figure out how to survive the bullies next year. I was doing my best Scarlet O'Hara impression, "I'll think about it tomorrow."

There were so many nice kids and on balance, most all of our days were happy. Between my motorcycle to get away on, my dog to protect me, and the large attic bedroom I shared with my sister, I had some security against those few of ill will.

But I won't kid you, I spent a lot of time in my room reading and writing – "write lightly, yours truly, dear Diary," as the Moody Blues later sang – if the bullies were on the prowl. It seemed they lived two beaches over, but I never knew for sure. All I knew was Barbara was as big as a bull, as strong as an ox, and as nasty as old garbage. No question, she could definitely beat my ass if she could ever catch me alone.

During the school year, the bus stop, a few blocks from my house, had its share of hazards. There were the boys who would take my books, pull my hair, and this year they were trying to lift up my skirts. That's when I decided it was time for dance shorts under every single skirt.

The same two girls, Barbara Smitt and Lori – I never did know her last name – would, from time to time, come to our bus stop during the school year. Lori would hover nearby and glower at me while Barbara threatened me, if there weren't too many others nearby. What the fuck did I do to her?

The answer would come to me in later years, I had a loving home with lots of fun toys, like my motorcycle, which she clearly didn't have. I always saw her walking, never even on a bicycle, much less a motor bike. But mostly, I could avoid any confrontation with them by having Deb or Nancy with me – or Dad would just drive us to school.

So, if you are wondering how the writer narrating this story came to be, I need to thank a bully who terrified me into hiding in my room where I would read and write. Well, maybe not. She died of a heroin, horse, smack, junk, whatever you want to call it, overdose in later years. But we'll get back to that . . .

As I look behind on these moments with you, I see many things more clearly, and this one stands out. Our life was abnormal for the times and even the place. Dad bought and sold Beach real estate between shifts at the factory and farming. His two lawyers were Mr. Pines, the wonderful, fun, Black man that you've already met, and Mr. Bornstein, a friendly but reserved Jewish man, who was only a little upset when we toilet papered the trees in the front yard of his home.

Shit, I didn't even realize it was his house until way too late! After all, it was nighttime! He just told my dad what had happened and we cleaned it all up. But first, we got a serious talking-to. That settled it. Both Mr. Pines and Mr. Bornstein often visited us in our home and greatly enriched our lives.

With both our parents working, Henrietta, a wonderful Black woman, was often our caretaker over the years. Everyone called her Hank. Mostly, in the early years, she stayed inside the house and backyard. At the time, I thought little of the why....

She was the sister of Claire, who worked at Ford's with Mom. Hank worked at a factory with less union job security, that would often see layoff periods. That's when she would come help us for extra money. She was so much fun, a wonderful cook, a very talented seamstress, and so much more. She was our friend. Even better, she followed Daddy's instructions, "Tell them to do their homework, then just let the girls play, but watch over them," which gave us a lot of freedom.

With Mom in the UAW, she always got free passes to events. However, working the way she did, she would just toss them on the fireplace mantel and say, "Use them or give them away." Often, if we were looking for something to do, it would be Dad, Deb, and me or Dad, us and Hank who used the passes to events of interest. Maybe they were passes to the fairgrounds, car races, or festivals.

One Sunday, with Mom at work picking up overtime, the four of us decided to use the Cobo Arena passes on the mantel. Hank had been wanting to go. Dad said we could go shopping at the Hudson's Department Store afterwards. It was a beautiful day, but hot. We had all the windows down in the car, and the music on the radio was blaring. As we drove into the Detroit area, Dad suddenly turned the radio off, and the traffic became unbearable. Then we saw absolutely the largest crowd of people I had ever seen.

We heard singing as hundreds of people were walking and clapping. The police were everywhere, just watching. It was almost like some sort of massive mobile outdoor church service with security provided by the city. We could clearly see Dad was getting more than a little nervous from being stuck in the massive traffic jam. We knew better than to cause a ruckus at a time like that, so we remained quiet as mice in the back seat as he and Hank looked for a way out of the gridlock

While Dad was looking for a place to pull the car over, he asked Hank, "What the hell is going on? It's just a rally. I didn't expect it to be this crowded." Hank said, "You need to leave me here and take the girls home. It's not safe. I'll get a ride back." Dad was looking for a place to turn around while talking to Hank. He said, "I knew King would draw a crowd, but I didn't expect this!" Hank smiled as she gathered her purse to exit the car.

Deb called out from the back seat, "I want to go with Hank!" I chimed in, "Me, too!" Hank turned to Dad and us, "Absolutely not. I'll tell you all about it." Dad looked at us in the back seat, "No damn way!" Then he turned to Hank, "You sure you can get a ride back?" Hank nodded. Dad said, "If not, call me. I'll fight my way here to get you!"

Hank got out of the car and joined the immense crowd. Dad finally found a way to turn the car around and head toward home, with his two very pissed off daughters in the back seat. It was June 23, 1963, and the day of "The Great Freedom March" of Rev. Dr. Martin Luther King, Jr.

In the days to come, Hank would tell us all about the event. Even though she had a pass to get inside, the packed crowd prevented her from getting close enough to enter Cobo Arena. She stood outside with thousands of others as the prelude to the "I Have a Dream" speech was broadcast to the crowd.

Berry Gordy from Motown would record this event. It would not be long before we would hear that very speech. It was the one that captivated the world – that was the speech that Hank was able to hear in person!

CHAPTER SIX

Nothing about any of this was "normal," but it was our normal. Most everyone around accepted our way of life in the Beaches, with grace. If not, they just kept their "damn mouth shut," as Mom often suggested to some of them. That was just how my mother handled assholes, pure and simple.

The Beaches were filled with teenagers – some were boys and girls who lived in the few larger homes that were far from mansions, and others came from small, well-kept cottages. Then there were some who were simply dirt poor, with junk filling their yards – just living on the margin. None of us could ever be defined as rich; these were working-class people. People with one income, two incomes or maybe not much of an income at all.

All of this I wouldn't understand until many years later. After all, Deb and I were just kids who, thankfully, were living a good life. For us everything was easy – if someone else we knew was hungry, we would feed them. In the summer, with most parents at work, the Beach kids' freedom was plentiful.

Town, only a few miles away from the Beaches communities, was filled with shops like Klines that carried the best bellbottom jeans, restaurants like the lunch counter at S.S. Kresge's or Cunningham's, a big pool hall, a record store, and more. Also, some of the town boys were really quite cute. We'd always find plenty of town kids to play with and fun adventures to be had. In town, they even had an armory that held live band events.

Deb and I spent all day one Saturday getting dressed for a concert and dance contest at the Armory. I had my long hair waved out and wore a long red V-neck t-shirt dress with bell sleeves. Clearly, my outfit was rocking every curve I had. Dad dropped us off for music and dancing to live music.

The band was still setting up when we arrived – that was part of our plan. We walked up next to the stage to talk and flirt with the musicians. One of the band members was wearing a fantastic turquoise belt. I told him, "That belt would look great with this dress!" He flippantly replied, "You be the best dancer tonight and maybe it's yours."

Now I say flippantly, because he was wearing a very expensive belt and the prize for the dance contest was a small cheap trophy. However, naïve me took it to heart and grabbed the best dancer in town, Christian Berkley. We were magnificent on that dance floor, if I do say so myself. No surprise – we won. The trophy was given out after the dance, and it was handed to Christian. I told him he could keep it. However, I was bummed when I discovered, Bob Seger and his turquoise belt had already left the building.

The events that were happening and the places to go in town were very different from what went on in the Beaches. At the Beaches, we had an ice cream parlor, a small grocery store, a pizza parlor – a great one, a bakery, a meat market with peperoni sticks that were strung over a clothesline at the ceiling, a couple of restaurants, and a grand skating rink. The skating rink was where you would find us hanging out every Sunday.

No, I didn't have to go to church first. I had already received what I thought was a complete Baptist religious education by age twelve. It even included attendance at summer Bible School, for crying out loud! Although my grandfather helped to build one of the larger Baptist churches, the demand for our mandatory presence and tithes – a Latin word for levy or tax money – had been declared null and void by both of our parents.

Once my parents felt we had learned the basics of the religion, had our bible book, and were baptized, we could decide for ourselves. We were no longer required to attend church the way my mother had been forced into daily, even sometimes twice a day or more, church attendance in the south.

Dad, although he was baptized late in life, was more of a spiritual man than a participant in organized religion. To each their own – that was my parents' true philosophy. However, from time to time my mother, who needed extra sleep and seeking quiet, would demand my father take us to church before we could go skating. On many occasions, he would tell us, "Leave your tithe money when you go inside and come out the back door. I'll be back to pick you up."

Yes, there he would be, waiting to take us to the Golden Drumstick Diner for lunch, or somewhere else to kill the time until Mom had her rest and it was safe for us to go home. As we entered the car, a scant three minutes after entering the church, he would say two things, "Girls, you make sure God always comes to your house; and no matter what, don't tell your mother what you did!" So, if you think we had a co-conspirator in life, you're entirely right – it was our dad.

One Sunday, Dad wanted to go see Mr. Pines, "Maybe we can all grab a steak at the diner." As we drove across the track and into the east side of town, Dad saw Mr. Pines' bright red Cadillac at another home; the yard was filled with people. Dad pulled over. As he got out, he said, "Wait here a minute. It looks like he may be busy."

Mr. Pines saw Dad as he approached and joined him partway through the yard. They talked for a second and then Mr. Pines waved and called out to us, "Come on!" Deb and I jumped out of the car in excitement. Dad laughed as he told us, "Go on – there are hot dogs and hamburgers on the grill." Deb had been complaining that she was starving in the car. We raced toward the grills full of food.

As we loaded our plates, we noticed a group of men strumming guitars and singing old Baptist hymns. A big group of people were sitting around them. Deb and I headed over and sat down on the ground. We were taught to leave chairs for the elderly, but to be honest, there was not one empty chair anyway.

The men finished the song. As they were just laughing and talking for a minute, Deb said, "Recognize that man on the end? Come on." She jumped up and I followed her. As we approached the man, Deb quickly said, "You're Chuck Berry! You wrote, 'Sweet Little Sixteen.' I'm sixteen and I just love that song!" Mr. Berry smiled and he looked to another man standing nearby, "Elijah, we got one?" Then he began to play "Sweet Little Sixteen," seated, which was amazing to see.

Elijah headed off and I could see him at the trunk of a car parked nearby. When he returned and Mr. Berry finished the song to the roar of the partygoers, he handed the 45 RPM record to Mr. Berry, who handed it to Deb, "What's your name? Deb smiled, "Deb, and this is my little sister, Claudette. Thank you!" Then the men returned to playing music, but shifted to blues.

Later that day in the car, with both of us too excited to be quiet, Dad said, "We're going to have to tell your mom we skipped church. No way we'll be able to keep this quiet from your mom!" Deb looked at Dad, "Well, like the Catholics, we'll go to confession and take the heat!" Dad laughed, "You mean I'll take the heat!"

As Dad dropped us off at the skating rink, Deb handed him the record, "Take care of this!" Dad laughed, "I'll tell your mom all about it. I can already feel her wrath! Pick you up right around six."

That record played for a long time at home. Now and then, Mom would laugh and say, "Church, huh?" Deb always regretted that she had gotten so excited that she didn't think to ask him to sign it!

Our Sundays at the skating rink revolved around friends, roller-skating, round frozen pizzas that tasted like cardboard, and more. Round and round we'd go, with loud music, a large mirrored ball above our heads, and flashing lights filling our day.

We latched onto one another's hands in the early days, as we were learning how to skate. We did our first spins in skating outfits, with pompoms tied to our skates. Yet, before our last spins in this utopia, we had replaced our childhood attire. By that time, denim bell bottom jeans and fringed cowhide jackets adorned our adolescent bodies.

The idea was to skate as fast as you could, until you would most likely get the ultimate badge of honor – the penalty box. It seemed the penalty box was mostly filled with boys. Like most everywhere in our lives, it was mainly the boys who got in trouble at the skating rink. Although the girls had their share of time in "the box," too. Kara, one girl, seemed to join me there quite often. I'll never understand how my sister was able to escape penalty time. I told you – she was smart!

Kara Riggers was my age, my class in school, but much taller, a strongly built girl who hung out with the boys. She could skate as fast as us. Between Deb, Kara, and me, we never knew which would win the singles race. It seemed to be the luck of the draw; each of us was just that fast.

Often, Deb and I would run the double skating races with her pushing me, while I was in a crouched position. When the triple race came, Kara would often push Deb and me. I was always the leader in the train position, because I had great control on the turns. We were unstoppable! Kara was a really nice girl who never put on a front. I can tell you today, life turned out just fine for her.

Of course, we always had to be on the alert for the presence of bully Barbara. Thankfully, Lori never went with her to the skating rink. On the days that she was there, we had to watch our backs. After all, she was big enough to carry out all those threats she voiced. We always made sure she could never catch one of us alone. If one of us needed to head into the restroom, all three of us went together. That way, the worst we might face would be her taunts, but not her violence. She was an absolutely nasty piece of work, if you haven't figured that out already.

Saturday usually involved going the other direction on Dixie Highway – for a trip downtown. It was very different from life in the Beaches; the town had lots of red lights, crosswalks, and police. At home, we didn't need to watch out for speeding cars – they had to watch out for us. We knew we would lose some of our freedom in town, but it was fun for an afternoon. Besides, there were these two real cute brothers, but they were kind of stuck on themselves. After all, in their eyes, we were just "Beach girls." You know, not good enough for them, even though we had both overheard them mentioning more than once about how they thought those Sutton sisters were "cool."

We did everything we could think of, including resting on the grave markers at Memorial Place, a cemetery where soldiers from the War of 1812 are buried. We always positioned ourselves on a hill near the bed where plants spelled out "Monroe." Then we would rise up slowly, trying to scare people in passing cars. It never really worked, but we were sure it was a good idea.

Or maybe we'd climb the giant bronze statue of General Custer astride his horse located near the Rasin River. Please note here, I was never responsible for painting the balls of Custer's horse red, but I might know the name of a culprit or two....

One Saturday, I remember heading down the steps and into the town pool hall with Deb in front of me. I could hear what the older town boys were whispering as we descended the steps. These are the words I heard, "Look, here comes that Deb Sutton. Wow!" Then I heard another boy's voice saying, "If you think that's something, look behind her – that one's really exotic looking!"

I think this was the first time, despite all of the flaws I could see in my looks, that I came to the realization there might actually be something appealing about me. I knew that what my sister had in the looks department was very pleasing to a boy's eye, but that whispered comment I overheard about me came as an enormous surprise.

Deb looked like Dad's mother, who carried the bloodline of Alexander Hamilton, several generations before her in the family tree. I looked like my mother and her heritage of past generations of Indians. Dad called us Vanilla and Chocolate. I really don't think that area lacked in pretty girls or handsome boys, but it was nice to be noticed.

We always seemed to call Dad earlier than planned to come pick us up from town. Our love for the Beaches was more than clear. In time, others would be able to figure out just how much we cared.

Our big bedroom was the entire top of the house, rebuilt just for us by Dad and the brother-in-law of one of my mother's older children. That guy was one hell of a carpenter. The room was a well-furnished haven for us, with matching twin beds, a nice stereo, a small refrigerator, a desk, chairs, a TV, its own telephone extension, and more.

Our room was a great meeting place for the kids. The two large windows and Dads' emergency trellis next to them made for easy entrance and exit, even though that was against the rules. Music from The Beatles to The Beach Boys and so on filled the air, but for me it was Ottis Redding's "Dock of the Bay" that filled my soul. Deb was all in on Aretha Franklin's "Respect!"

By the beginning of summer, Deb was more interested in boys, but she wasn't over the top about them. There wasn't any special guy in her life. I liked one or two boys a little more than as friends, but neither of us girls were even considering having sex, and it seemed like that was all most of the boys were interested in at that age. Since they were still calling me "tight-legs," I was far from their first choice as a girlfriend candidate.

The good thing was that they didn't even lie about having sex with me – at least, as far as I know. I think they fabricated their tales about most of the girls they claimed to have laid. But who knows? Like I said, it's the girls who hear and spread the rumors.

Deb was always thinking and talking about problems in the world. She seemed too intent on solving them all – single-handedly, no less. But, after all, she was still a teenage girl and thoughts of boys were never far from her mind. One particular day, she was busy drying her hair with her hands, her head hanging out the open window. She was clearly getting ready to go somewhere. On the bed was her peasant blouse with the Angela Davis pin, bell bottom jeans and just below the bed on the floor, her heeled boots.

Noticing all her primping, and being anxious to fulfill my role as her often annoying little sister, I asked, "Got a date?" She smiled and coyly said, "His name is Ronnie and I met him at Sharon's party last night on the other Beach." Sharon Wates, seventeen, was a longtime friend of Deb's. She was a smart girl, but she didn't much like me hanging around with Deb and her.

When I learned there was a boy involved, I grinned at Deb. She smiled at me, saying, "Don't get too excited, Yeah, he's cute and all, but more important to me is that he thinks and how he thinks. You know, about important stuff – like civil rights! That's all we talked about last night. He's been marching with us, but I never saw him before last night. He told me he's been watching me at the protests and he knew right then that he wanted to meet me. Really, I can't believe it – he was there, right in front of my eyes all the time, but I never even saw him until the party."

Nancy was far more interested in things about Deb's boyfriend other than his mind and exclaimed, "Spill! Gimme the dirt!" Deb wouldn't, saying, "You two – scat!" Turning a deaf ear to her, I changed the record and "California Dreaming" started playing. Deb ignored us both and continued to dry her hair.

That was, until she needed something. "Hey, Ette, ask Dad to drop us off downtown in a couple of hours." I smirked, "Sure." Nancy quickly jumped in, "Yes! You got it!" Deb returned to drying her hair, hanging her head back out of the window.

The bedroom phone rang, I answered, "Hello? Really! We're on the way." I hung up, grabbed Nancy's hand, and pulled her with me. "Something's happened at the lake. Come on!" Deb, not even a little fazed by the call, continued doing her thing. We, on the other hand, raced out of the house and down the road to the lake.

CHAPTER SEVEN

A summer mist of rain didn't deter us as we rushed down the street and across the grassy knoll. As we approached the beach that day, we saw a small group of boys off in the distance. When the two of us reached the long breakwall, we jumped off it near the middle. We landed on the sand near the water's edge, and walked toward the boys.

Johnny was always dressed for winter, even in summer. From his suede fringe jacket with no shirt and long pants to his sweatshirt hoodies, he was a strange boy. With him were Joey Larmar, fifteen, who was rough around the edges but harmless to the girls, and Mike Grant. Mike was seventeen, a tall boy with a mean spirit, who had arrived at the Beaches just that year. I preferred not to be alone around him. Both were followers of Johnny.

The rain stopped and the sun came out, shining brightly. All three boys were standing on the sand near the lake's edge, but far down the breakwall from us. They weren't too far back from police crime scene tape. We raced down the sand by the water's edge to where they were talking and gawking.

Mike stepped back and up onto the breakwall for a closer look, "Looks like a murder! That's a body they're covering." We could see some of the action within the taped off area; the big blue tarp was being placed over something. Nancy asked, "Could it be a drowning? Can you recognize who it is?" Mike stretched to see more, "Can't tell."

I looked over to the far side of the crime scene and saw my dad talking with the police over by the yellow tape. At that moment, he saw us. With the wave of his hand stretched out from his mighty long arm, he motioned with his big hand, finger pointing to the direction of home. My dad was very even-tempered with us kids, but when he looked down over the top of his glasses and motioned a second time, I knew it was time for us to go.

The boys absolutely refused to move. Johnny made that crystal clear, "Fuck no – I'm staying!" Because the boys wouldn't leave, I had to pull Nancy away. The two of us moved back a long way and sat near the middle of the breakwall, about where we had jumped onto the beach. I knew that we'd hear all about the crime shortly and for weeks more, until it just became old news.

Often, as I traveled all over this country and lived far away, I'd read in a newspaper or on the internet about a murder in this little area just outside of Detroit. I never seem to hear about cases being solved. To this very day, it bothers me. It's not like this town is New York or LA! Maybe unsolved cases everywhere strike at my core, because I remember the lake cases of a time long past.

Anyway, it wasn't long before we saw the police chasing the boys our way. I think Johnny had a warrant out on him for breaking and entering, so we all took off for the shack. A couple of streets behind my house there stood a well-known shack behind the trees and tall weeds overgrown long ago. Among the Beach kids it was quite well known; it was our haven. We had all made it into our own little clubhouse, with pillows, candles, a few old broken chairs, and plenty of rocks and tree stumps outside to sit on.

Before long, the area near the shack was filled with fifteen or twenty kids. Not one of them knew a thing about what had really happened on the beach. Cigarettes and joints came out of their pockets as smoke filled the air. The lack of information didn't stop the conspiracy and murder theories from flying!

Nancy was the first. "It's a girl, right?" Johnny followed with, "Looked like a guy to me." Then Mike took his position of pride in the middle of the group, "I was standing up higher! I could see more. It's a girl with long brown hair – she was murdered. I heard them say murder!" I quickly chimed in with, "Girl? You were too far away to see anything well, and we couldn't hear shit. No way!"

Nancy laughed and whispered to me, "At least we know it's not Deb's Ronnie." Of course, there was no way we could know whether or not Ronnie was the body on the beach at that point. Nancy's non sequitur told me she was still really curious about this guy Ronnie, fascinated with the one who had caught Deb's eye. He was still on her mind! The kids went on arguing over male or female, drowning or murder. This is how the whole afternoon would go, while we waited to hear some real facts.

Hours passed, as most of the kids smoked pot and cigarettes. The smoke filled the area and even the nonsmokers must have been stoned. Time after time, someone would just conjure up another stoned story about what could've happened. After a few hours, we all agreed to head off and find some facts to bring back to the group. We'd meet up later.

Back at the house, Dad was resting in the easy chair for his midnight shift at the paper mill, which, by the way, started at 10 p.m. So, no news from him, at least for a while. Deb had found her own ride into town. It really wasn't too hard; we didn't have to hitch-hike often. We'd just walk toward the entrance to the Beaches and a passing neighbor headed to town would give us a ride.

Nancy and I were watching TV when we saw a car through the front window. A really cool black 1964 Chrysler Imperial was pulling up. We could see a guy was driving. He just dropped Deb off and left in a hurry. He even kicked up a little dust on the road.

We raced to the door. But alas, Ronnie and the car were gone. Deb was smiling as she told us, "I told him to do that so you couldn't bother us!" Not happy that we didn't get to meet him, I told her, "Speeding in here – Dad sure won't welcome that!" Nancy chirped in,

"Who cares? I just want to get a really good look at him and sit in that gorgeous car!"

As Deb reached the front porch, she told Nancy, "They're both hot!" Before we went in, I told her, "Dad's sleeping." We all entered the cottage foyer quietly. The foyer was like a second porch, only enclosed in glass.

Quickly, but whispering, we let her know there was a murder at the beach. At first, she didn't believe us. It's only when I said, "Wake Dad and ask him," that she knew I was telling the truth. We didn't wake Dad unless it was a real emergency. He worked a swing shift, days, afternoons, and midnights. That way, he could be home with us kids as much as possible. That schedule meant he would sleep whenever he could catch a few hours.

I remember one time, the pink plug-in princess phone with the long cord, the one downstairs in the living room, kept ringing for us girls. Some of the boys called over and over and played The Beatles song, "Michelle, Ma Belle." I could hear them giggling. My dad was so mad he hopped up and unplugged the phone, then tossed it like a baseball, as hard as he could, out the front door. By the time the phone landed in the yard, it was smashed.

89

Dad was devastated at what he had just done. "I'm so sorry, but I'm just over-tired. I shouldn't have done that." I told him, "Dad, it was ringing off the hook." He told me, "That's no excuse. Come on, let's go get a burger and a new phone." Dad stayed up after that and went to work with no sleep.

So anyway, with Dad asleep this day, Deb motioned to me, whispering, "The kitchen." We headed into the small cottage kitchen and took a seat at the metal table with the red vinyl-back chairs. We quickly filled her in on the details (of which we knew nothing) and asked, "You know her?"

Deb seemed concerned, but said, "Don't know, that's a pretty vague description you're giving me, a boy or a girl, maybe with brown hair. From that, I can't tell anything at all. Are you sure it's really a murder and not just an accidental drowning?" Nancy said, "You bet!" But I quickly told Deb, "No, we're not sure." Deb decided to wait for the news or for Dad to wake up to get the scoop.

When he awoke, Dad was able to give us a few facts. He told us it was an unknown girl with long brown hair, wearing a flowered shirt. She had drug track marks, but there was something in clear view that told the police it was a murder. When it came to drugs, Dad always told us the dark side of the story, and that reassured him that we'd never be foolish enough to mess with hard drugs.

He wouldn't tell us the details of the violence surrounding her death. All he would say was that the police were sure she was murdered. No one knew who she was and the cops thought her body floated on the currents from somewhere close to the Enrico Fermi Nuclear Generating Station. Everybody just called it "the Fermi."

Did I mention, the Beach is three miles from a large nuclear power plant? It's a plant that a few years ago was being looked at for radiation leaks and possibly causing higher than normal cancer rates in the area. Of course, back in the mid-60s, none of us knew a tremendous amount about the long-term effects of even slight radiation exposure.

Like us, it was located halfway between Detroit and Toledo. Construction began in 1956, but it reached criticality and went online in 1963. In 1966, a boiler was added, and there was a partial meltdown in what they called Fermi 1 because of a liquid sodium leak into

91

the reactor. That made some folks nervous, but not everyone.

That was only the year before our summer of '67, so repair contractors from all over the world were working there. No big shock -- the Fermi was on everybody's minds. We're talking about an actual nuclear power plant meltdown – you know, people – uranium!

Even though we were all living only a few miles from a thousand-acre nuclear facility, the Fermi brought jobs. In an industrial area like Detroit, job creation is always the first consideration. It had come first before factory runoff polluted Lake Erie, and again before everyone was exposed to radiation and heavy water leakage from the Fermi.

When I was visiting my half-sister at her house one day, she calmly told me she never worried about an explosion at Fermi. She used to say, "If it ever happens, we're so close we won't feel a thing." Now you know.

The whole area was overrun by transient contract workers, but they weren't allowed to hang out in the Beaches. That is, all but one real nice guy Dad rented a house to. His name was Matt Gardner, and he was thirty-five and outrageously handsome. With his long, tall frame, expensive clothes, and gentle voice, he was a sight to behold and a pleasure to be with. Naturally, he always drove an absolutely perfect 1960s black Jaguar.

Matt climbed the towers at the Fermi. The higher the risk, the more you got paid. Matt's job was one of the riskiest. I kind of had a crush on him, not that I let on to anyone.

Dad trusted him enough to let him give me a ride in the Jag once. Matt was always a complete gentleman and I'm sure he only thought of me as a little kid. Even though he worked for a contractor at Fermi, I was sure he had nothing to do with the murder. In fact, I found out he was in California visiting family when it happened. So, not guilty!

For a while, all the rage was talk about a deranged killer on the loose. A story was going around about some nameless girl who was seen at a downtown protest rally and then got herself killed. Rumors about the death of this young girl would fade away, then just pop back up every now and then.

CHAPTER EIGHT

On the small black and white TV in our bedroom, the network news was broadcasting stories of people protesting all around the country. We didn't get a lot of channels, but we could get the three major networks. I was completely captivated by the network news. The news seemed to take me prisoner and it wouldn't release its massive grip.

Much older boys we knew casually were coming home from the war. They were the older brothers of kids we knew, mostly from town. Most of them were maybe six or seven years older than we were. They seem so different from the kids we knew before they left for war. We saw complete strangers in the boys we were friendly with before. Their facial expressions often had a faraway look in their eyes. They'd talk to us for a social hello and move on. It was like they no longer knew us – or they no longer cared.

I'd hear on the news that someone died in the war in Southeast Asia. I had asked teachers about the war before school ended that year, but they failed to answer my questions. I asked Dad, but even his answers were vague. He'd quickly tell Deb, "It may be best if Claudette doesn't watch the news. It could give her nightmares." I think I've already made it clear, but just to be sure you get it, I was the baby of the family, spoiled and protected. Lucky me.

Nancy wasn't interested in the war. She seemed to be missing a lot. It was like I barely saw her. She had started dropping acid with the boys and a few girls. Deb was gone so much I could barely get anything out of her except at night. When we were alone in our room, she'd talk a bit before she slept. Deb liked her sleep, hence the BB gun in the ass.

So, all alone with a low light in the corner, I'd search on my own for answers about the war and everything else about the world. I used a large set of World Book Encyclopedias Dad bought us and the newspapers we were able to check out of the public library and the bookmobile. Of course, I'd watch the TV news in our room, making sure the sound was so low that no one else could hear.

In one of the short story sections of my World Books, I read one about an orphan girl who got her braids cut off. I think it was called, "You Must Be Punished." I'd dream about that and the threat for the coming school year by my bullies. I was quite unsettled those days. Nothing seemed right – and how right I was about that!

So many things I wanted to know! Where was Southeast Asia? Where was Vietnam? Why were we fighting there? What are Civil Rights? I had all of these and a million other questions. I felt they all should have been answered at school, but they weren't. So, I would search for answers in the pages . . .

The region's Vietnam War Memorial had just been dedicated. The nightly news had begun carrying footage from the war zone. I still didn't understand it all. As it would turn out, the lyrics of songs would help me find answers, or shall I say, a big dose of reality.

Living just outside of Motown had its advantages. One was that we would often hear about some new music coming, pre-release. Maybe it was the name of a new band, word that a band was releasing a new album or song, a song title, or a lyric line that would spread via the rumor mill. Some would be made up, but from time to time, the grapevine bore fruit.

In Detroit, a recording studio called "Hitsville USA" and a label called Motown created music that would become the score for the civil rights movement. It brought Black images and talent into homes all across the nation. That music introduced Black music and culture to the baby boomer generation of White kids. Some of the greatest talents of a generation like Marvin Gaye, The Four Tops, The Supremes, Smokey Robinson, Stevie Wonder, Gladys Knight and the Pips, and many more called Motown their home.

So, to say our music grapevine was good isn't an understatement. When I heard a line on the Motown vine about an upcoming song to be released out of New York City by a band from Berkley, I knew it was the real thing. That line stuck in my head then and still resonates today. As it turned out, the line I heard was from "The Vietnam Song," by Country Joe and The Fish. It carried possibly the most powerful image of war in words ever written: "Be the first one on your block, To have your boy come home in a box."

This line set the pace of the anti-war movement for me. You know, they say a little knowledge is a dangerous thing. We all had fragments of the truth and believed we knew all the answers. I think that it was the same for the boys who enlisted. Some thought they understood what war was and what they were getting into because their fathers had fought in World War II or Korea. Some had no idea, but just followed. Like I said, there are always leaders and followers.

The signs at the peace marches reading, "No More Bombs" is a perfect example of blind ignorance. We couldn't understand how those bombs that were being dropped in Vietnam wouldn't hit our soldiers. What we didn't know was that those bombs were often providing ground cover for our soldiers. Nor did we grasp when our radio operators on the ground called in strikes from ships in the ocean, white phosphorous munitions were used as a target marker for the strike.

Whether you agree or disagree with the rationale for why we were fighting a war in Southeast Asia, I can only tell you this: we as America fight wars elsewhere to keep war from our shores. It's a matter of maintaining the balance of world power. In this case, Communist China had a great interest in Vietnam and Cambodia. If you think for one moment that American soldiers' presence in Vietnam started in the 1960s, you're sadly mistaken. We had a military presence there from the early 1950s.

In the end, at least 58,220 American soldiers would die. Over 150,000 more would receive clearly visible, life-changing injuries. Approximately 1,600 were listed as POWs – prisoners of war, or MIA – missing in action. Hundreds of thousands would carry the internal scars of a war that finally ended with the Fall of Saigon … to communism.

Deb had become a regular participant at a joint protest originally called, "The Protest for Racial Equality and Peace." By then, these had grown to full blown "Anti-War" protests from California to Detroit.

Deb's signs for the marches were stacked in a large cubbyhole of our bedroom designed for extra storage. I spoke not a word of them to our parents. In return, Deb would bring me newspapers. Kids came from different cities around the country to march. They brought their local papers to swap. For me, this was a gold mine.

The San Francisco Oracle told me all about the "Summer of Love" and the "Hippie Movement." It said that over 85,000 young people found a new home in San Francisco's Haight-Ashbury district. Everybody there was looking for a communal way of life through art, music, peace, love, and the beauty of their surroundings in northern California. There were pictures of girls with flowers in their hair. Nice news – for a change.

Back then, I saw a Chicago Tribune column about a deadly chemical that the US military was spraying in Vietnam. How could this not get on our soldiers? Different news – not so nice. Years later, I would come to understand that chemical was called "Agent Orange." It was named after the color of the stripe on the barrels. Millions of gallons of herbicide chemicals were shipped over for spraying the foliage of Vietnam.

Several other deadly chemicals for spraying the fields and jungles came with different colored stripes on their barrels. Eventually, they would collectively become known as Agent Orange. As I suspected then, the chemical(s) would get on our soldiers and even be bad for the women and children of Southeast Asia. Sadly, our boys came home with internal physical damage to their organs from Agent Orange. Their injuries still keep showing up, even decades later. Like I said, it may be that we knew too little, but we kids were right sometimes.

That hot summer, Ronnie became Deb's steady. He was a really sweet and very funny seventeen-year-old boy. Tall, handsome, and thin, he made everyone smile. He would pick Deb up for the marches. They were as thick as thieves together in the anti-war and civil rights movements. Deb was in love – little sisters can tell these things, you know.

Usually, the transportation for the protest was a car full of people, generally after Mom and Dad had gone to work. However, if one of our parents was home, Deb would slip out the back. Then she'd come around the side of the house where I had dropped her protest signs from the bedroom window. She'd pick them up on her way.

After she was out of the house and had collected her signs, she'd run through the backyard, through our garage, and then she'd arrive on the next street to meet Ronnie and whoever was in the car with him. Our home was on one street, the fenced yard behind led to the garage, followed by a driveway and another gate. That gate abutted the next street. That layout was perfect for sneaking out!

From time to time, I'd make her take me to a rally, under threat of telling Mom and Dad what she was really doing. Blackmail among sisters is quite fun and very commonplace – at least it was for us. Some things held a lot of power. But as with anything, they would only work for so long.

The marches in Detroit were all so big, with signs saying, "Stop The War," "Stop The Bombs," "Civil Rights For All," and "My Body"! It was a fascinating time of change in America and around the world. People were there from every walk of life – and both young and old showed up.

It seemed like a million people to me, all talking about different things – their voices were so loud. In reality, I would sit on the grass and try to count all the marchers. I got to about one hundred and seventy-five the first time, two hundred-fifty at the second rally, and the third and last time, I lost count at well over three hundred.

I say the last time, because Deb finally called my bluff. She said, "It's too dangerous for you to be there. I can't keep track of you and do the work. So, tell Dad if you want, but I won't stop!" That was it, at least for a while.

The look on my face told her I wouldn't tell. With a hug, her tender voice in my ear said, "Cover for me. That's an important job, too!" I pulled back, locked my stretched-out arms against her shoulders, and without hesitation told her, "Go forth, young woman. I've got your back!" Deb smiled and said, "We're going all over this country! Now I need to make some flyers to tell people where we'll be marching next."

My immediate reply was, "I can do that!" Deb smiled, "Sure, Kiddo, that's another great job for you. But you're at home for now. Maybe soon, it'll be safe to take you back." Except for "Spock," Deb gave me the only two nicknames I ever had, "Ette," and "Kiddo." I doubted she'd ever take me again; I could tell when she was worried about me.

But I did help the cause by typing using carbon paper, and writing with markers – everything for posters and flyers. Did I mention my father was a papermaker? All I had to say was I needed some typing paper and a bunch of cardboard.

We even recruited several of the Beach kids, all sworn to silence. One or two would come by most days. Girls like Linda, Jeanie,

Tiffany, Sandy, Carol, and more would show up. All of them were my age and fun to hang out with. In this same room, we had played with Barbies, had sleepovers, and truly gone from pillow fights to lipstick.

That summer, in that very same room we were making lots and lots of anti-war and civil rights protest signs and posters. We'd take turns coming up with slogans, making signs, nailing them to wooden handles, and typing location flyers, all while playing rock and roll music at high volume.

In due course, the flyers would be picked up to hand out all over town. All of this was happening upstairs while my parents were at work. The 45 RPM records that we had so carefully attached to the ceiling for décor would sometimes fall on our heads. We really hadn't mastered keeping them up there.

The first time I asked, Dad brought home a trunk full of paper and cardboard at the end of his very next shift. The next time it was, "Dad the other kids don't have paper or cardboard and I'm low." That night, a full pallet with reams of paper appeared in the garage and sheets of cardboard were stacked against the side wall.

The paper mill where my dad worked recycled old paper, cardboard, and all sorts of things to make new cardboard. It was common practice for workers to pay three dollars if they wanted a pallet of goods before it was milled into the water for pulp. After all, if kids are asking for paper ... what harm could they do?

Anything made of paper, my father could get. There was another plus for the neighbor girls who helped. For some unknown reason, the mill received pallets of expensive, blue-boxed French nylons in different shades and sizes. I would dish those out to the girls.

Nancy would stop by and pretend to help, then disappear. She had open access to the nylon boxes. After all, she was my friend, in good times and bad. By then, I was sure she was drinking too much booze, smoking pot and doing acid. Far worse would come soon. I knew no one could stop her – I really had tried. At least, the signs kept me busy between bi-weekly threatening calls from our local bully. What did this bitch do, calendar me?

It was about this time that Dad was in full swing on renovations to the green house. Deb and I were playing outside the house one day, when Mr. Pines arrived. The two men sat in lawn chairs on the porch, talking. Of course, we were surreptitiously listening in on their entire conversation.

"The house is looking good, Mack." Dad nodded. "Yeah, it's getting there. But I'm almost wishing I hadn't bought it with that girl killed at the lake. She was a junkie, but the bound hands and feet meant she was alive when they put her in the water. We both know this area's getting to be full of drugs."

Mr. Pines looked to Dad, "They're looking at some workers from an out-of-state contractor. That's all I know. It worries me, too. But I'll tell you now, we got some serious trouble in Detroit. The potential for riots is growing, what with both racial and anti-war protests filling the streets up there. It's just a question of which one boils over first."

Dad shook his head. "You still going up to defend the Civil Rights marchers?" Mr. Pines shrugged. "Yeah, I was there last week and got a few out of jail. It's tense there – and I'm Black!" Dad looked really concerned. "You think it's gonna spill over to here?" Mr. Pines nodded, and Dad said, "What? You're Black!" Mr. Pines laughed a mirthless laugh. He stood up as he said, "Yeah, I'm as black as the ace of spades and this Black man sure is worried! Just be prepared to protect your property and your family."

Mr. Pines sat back down as he continued, "White supremacists from Toledo are scoping out this town, so it could be Black on White, White on Black – right here." Mack looked over his glasses, "My plan is never far. You know that hidden panel in the house?" Pines laughed, "Yep." Dad stood as well. He told Mr. Pines, "We've gotta stick together; make a plan to protect our families. Come on inside – I've got an idea." Dad got up and both men walked into the house. It was obvious that they didn't want us to hear more. I suppose that we weren't as surreptitious as we thought.

Later that day, the boys and Nancy were tossing pebbles at my bedroom window. It was our signal, so I headed out to meet them. We all took off toward the lake. Billy was throwing stones in the air and talking, "Hear any more about the girl in the lake?" I actually had some news. "Yeah, they're looking for somebody who is working for an out-of-state contractor." Johnny, surprised I had heard something he hadn't, asked, "Where'd you hear that?" With my best look of superiority I said, "Dad's lawyer, Mr. Pines."

Johnny never liked to be outdone. With a sneer he asked, "What's he know?" Then Johnny went on one of his standard racist tirades. A year earlier, I tried to explain the genesis of the word he was so fond of using just to piss me off. It was first used in the eighteen hundreds by White people to terrorize Black travelers. Johnny didn't seem to want to understand anything, other than stealing. Why he had a group of followers was beyond my ken.

Furious, I told Johnny, "Mr. Pines knows a hell of a lot more than you! I'm out of here!" Johnny said, "Don't go, I know that pisses you off, sorry – kind of." Still angry, I was determined to leave him with, "Shit mouth! Later guys – Nancy, you coming?" We both headed back to my house. The boys weren't getting what they wanted, so they started their usual duck arm flapping while calling, "cluck, cluck, cluck!"

Everybody with a lick of sense knew that neither of those two boys was a rocket scientist candidate. We were both used to Johnny and we realized things would never change with him. Yet, others seemed willing to follow his lead. In the end, that would be deadly for many.

CHAPTER NINE

The Fourth of July always had parties going on at the different beaches. It was a time for grills and smokers filled with food, beer, families, water and sun. Mom and Dad were grilling at the beach and had invited Claire and her twin girls, who were about three years old. The toddlers were sitting on a blanket in the sandy area. Everyone was watching them closely, so they didn't slip away and drown or get themselves into some other kind of dangerous situation.

The twins wanted to go in the water, so Claire and Dad took them to the water's edge. Suddenly, some of the families moved out of the water and started whispering on the shore. What the hell did they think – that the water would turn black?

Since their movement was more than obvious, Claire brought the kids back to the blanket. Dad followed her, angry as hell; he certainly wasn't speaking quietly when he said, "Stupid, ignorant son of a bitches!"

Mom tried to calm him for a second, then she held out a bottle of soda as she said to Claire, "Hold my Faygo! Mack, come on!" My mother gave the twins their sand buckets from the blanket. Then she, who did not like being in the water – actually, was petrified of swimming – took their hands and walked them to the water's edge. She sat down where the water and sand met and loudly pronounced, "Now you kids go ahead and play. Claire, come on down!" Dad stood tall over all four.

Not a whisper more was heard on shore. After a few minutes, most everybody who had gotten out of the water re-entered it. Those who left weren't missed – at least, not by any of us. I was often proud of my parents, but this day, especially so. As Dad would say, "Simple human kindness – if you learn nothing from your old dad, learn that."

Later that day, while all of the kids and parents were eating, Mom asked Claire if the layoff had hit Hank. "Yes, she's out for a while." Mom tried not to smile, "I hate to hear she's out. I know we don't pay as much as the factory, but we could sure use her to look after the girls. We just don't like leaving them alone, not even for a few hours between our shifts. I'll pay her by the week."

Claire laughed, "She told me to ask if you needed her!" You could see the relief in my mother's face, "Lordy! As soon as she can start! Never you mind, I'll call her the minute we get back home."

She turned to Dad, Deb and me and called out, "We got Hank!" Everyone loved when she took care of us – our parents didn't have to worry about their girls and we had a great time with Hank. With everyone around us hearing Mom's announcement, they all knew Hank was going to be coming back. To the kids, she baked, cooked, and took no crap from Johnny. Who, by the way, ate more than his fair share of her cookies – in fact, more than I could even count.

I'd always mess with Johnny when he was eating, "You know Hank baked those herself – with her own two hands!" Johnny, between bites would say, "Yeah, yeah I know, but they're so good!"

I don't think I told you, Claire and Hank were both in their mid-thirties, about five foot ten, built like brick shithouses and their skin was this beautiful shade of blue-black. We helped sew emerald and silver sequins on a mini-dress for Hank that summer. She would certainly look absolutely beautiful when she wore it out on a date.

Hank had a great sense of humor. Once, she cut her hand in the kitchen and said, "Look here, girls – my blood's red, too." Deb grinned as she replied, "What do you think – you're some-kind of a royal blue blood?" God, we certainly did love her.

Later that Fourth of July night, Mack and the guys set off fireworks lighting up the sky for all to enjoy. It was something my dad never had as a child, and he was determined to make sure we all did. Every year, he'd spend hundreds and hundreds of dollars purely for the entertainment of everyone.

The fireworks were followed by lighting the campfire for the kids after-party. The food and fun were over for the parents. It was the kids' time, with campfires on the beach and usually radios turned up as loud as they could go without breaking up.

As soon as all of the parents cleared out, Lori, the girl who hung out with bully Barbara, announced with an exaggerated wink and a nod, "Remember the warning, no alcohol, I'm the bartender tonight!" Deb was not happy,

"Lori, that's a booze call if I ever heard one. Aren't we supposed to be the older, more responsible ones?" Lori looked disgusted and called back to Deb, "Teetotaler! Who has any booze?" Bottles magically started to appear out of coolers.

Johnny and the boys had created a band and they were going to play on the beach. Matty's uncle, Sam Roberts, was forty-five, with a receding hair line and good heart. He worked with the Beach association a couple of Beaches over.

He and the boys put out plywood for a stage, plugged in their amps. We all listened as they blew the circuit breakers, again and again, just trying to set up. Finally, they gave up their big debut. No music tonight.

Then Uncle Sam, that's what we all called him, waved the boys over to the maintenance building. A few minutes later, they rolled out an old jukebox and Uncle Sam flipped the switch so we didn't need coins. As he was walking away, he said over his shoulder, "Have fun. I'll be back later to put it away."

With the jukebox blaring, kids talking, dancing in the sand, and doing some necking in the grassy knoll or near the water's edge, it had turned into a perfect night, despite its shaky musical start. That is until that Steve, from Nancy's mom's house, showed up. What an unmitigated creep!

Nancy had just arrived back at the party and she was really messed up. Alcohol, pills, weed – I had no idea what she was on. But she was barely able to talk, until she saw Steve. She gave him the finger and told him, "Get the fuck out of here!" Nancy was high as a kite, but when I say she was strong, she was tough!

Steve left just as Johnny was walking toward the group. Johnny asked Nancy if she needed anything. After only a few minutes, Nancy looked at Johnny and told him, "Come on!" They abruptly left the evening party right then. I didn't see her for several days.

Later, Barbara came by and pulled my braids, harassed other kids and me for a few minutes, before finally realizing that no one wanted her there. That night, there were a whole bunch of us but only one of her, so there was the real possibility of her being jumped and thumped by a number of kids. It sure wouldn't do for the Beach bully to be trounced by the very same kids she lived to torment. I'm certain that thought went through her head as she slithered away.

Late that night, I was introduced to a boy who had just moved to the Beach from France. Freddie Martin was his name. He was fifteen and very good looking, with darker skin like mine. He had beautiful sandy-colored hair, cut slightly longer, but well-styled. It highlighted his brown eyes.

Arriving at the party in nice shorts and a freshly pressed white shirt, he stood out. He spoke perfect English with a beautiful French accent and was very polite. At some point that evening, he asked if I wanted to go wading in the water's edge. We walked along the beach together and talked.

He was an only child. America felt very different for him and he knew he would have to work to fit in with the boys. It was the very first time that I really saw a boy without also imagining the word "Cooties" stamped right on his forehead.

He was smart, soft spoken, and not a thing like the rowdy boys I had grown up with. I mean, he didn't try to pull my hair, put his hand on my butt, or even take a peek down my shirt … that alone was a pleasant change. We were just two people walking and talking. We agreed to meet on the beach for another stroll the next morning. It made for an absolutely perfect ending to what had already been a fun Fourth of July.

We would continue meeting on the beach in the early mornings, walking and talking, as he adjusted to life in his new home. I'd answer questions about the boys and girls in the area, knowing that over time he'd end up making friends with the boys.

But for a while, he was my special friend, who eventually held my hand in the early morning hours as we strolled the beach. I liked him, or shall we say, I was suffering from a serious case of puppy love.

The very next day, all the kids would go camping in the Irish Hills. For us, Dad would drive a "Girls Only" camper up to the hills and set it up with food and supplies. It would house about twelve girls in very crowded conditions. Boys and girls from the town and the Beaches were all around in tents and sleeping bags. Dad was nobody's fool. "We're staying close by and I'll be checking in on you girls," he told us. We knew he meant it.

Campfires and live music would rock the acres of lush green hills, small towns, and surrounding lakes for two days. It was the prelude to the Goose Lake and Woodstock concerts. More than a few of the boys would try to slip into the camper whenever they could. Outside, the area was filled with multiple campfires. Around them, some kids were smoking pot, some drinking, while others were necking or trying to find a quiet place for sex.

This was the age of group status and mating rights. Which campfire circles would you be invited to join, which boy or girl would move over to give you a seat, and what group did you walk around in? For the girls, many aspired to join leaders like Becky Sand and her posse. They were mostly simply rude, just like her. But, then again, they were stuck in a tent – and I was in the cool camper.

Being snubbed seemed like a death sentence for some kids. So, even though we called out that the first seven more girls to come over could stay with us, they were too busy debating among themselves if we were worthy to act quickly. Before you knew it, we were full and they were still outside. Being superior was what occupied most of their time.

117

There were a few exceptions to the cliques – open groups like ours. We were having the best time. We'd swim, dance, laugh, and of course, check out the boys and vice versa!

For me it was all relatively harmless, a free-for-all with regular visits from Dad. He'd show up with lots of food, saying something like, "Just thought you girls would like some Kentucky Fried Chicken." Then he'd go in and check the camper for alcohol and pot. Finding none, he'd leave. We weren't stupid!

Freddie finally came to the hills for the first time on the last day, but he seemed too busy talking with the boys to seek me out. So, I just watched him from the camper window. Then, right before we left, he came by to talk to me for a few minutes. It made my weekend! I was sure he liked me.

My sister and Ronnie spent most of the weekend talking politics by the campfire with their like-minded friends, between necking sessions. I'd never met some of the people and they really didn't seem all that interested in having me around their political talk.

A few days after we returned home, Hank arrived. We were all settled in with her caring for us. Laughter filled the house and we were free to run. We just needed to be in by the time the street lights came on. Just like before, if we were late, Hank covered for us.

I was out on my motorcycle when I saw the screen door slam at Johnny's house. He raced out holding his face and crying, as his father was still cussing him. I could see he was running toward the shack. I was pretty sure what had just happened. I took my motorcycle home and grabbed a bag of frozen peas out of the garage freezer and walked over to the shack. As I approached, Johnny told me, "Get the fuck out of here!"

I walked up and sat down on the log next to where he was seated on the ground and handed him the bag of peas to put on his face. We sat there quietly together for a long time. After a while Johnny said, "You won't tell anybody at all, right?"

I told him, "I'll keep quiet about what I saw – but you need to do me a favor." I figured this was my best chance to get some peace and quiet for Hank. Johnny looked up, took the ice pack off his eye and said, "Sure. What?" I smiled and said, "Stop with the racist shit. Hank shouldn't have to put up with that."

Johnny smiled, "I'll try. Besides, she sure does make great cookies." Then he put the pack back onto his eye.

For the remainder of his black eye, and it was a bad one, Johnny told all the kids about the big fight he had in town with a boy, Johnny claimed he, "Beat his ass!" Of course, I knew that shiner came from his drunk father. But I spoke not a word and he backed off Hank.

A couple of weeks later, Gate told me that my sister had been arrested at a rally. I didn't believe him, and I made sure he knew it. "Liar! I'd know if my sister was arrested!" He told me, "Well, almost – if your dad hadn't come and gotten her out of the back of the cop car, she woulda been!" I stormed off, heading straight home to confront Deb. Sure enough, it turned out Gate was right – and she had been grounded for a few days. I just didn't know it.

She said, "I should've told you. But Dad was hot and he said not to." Then she went on to say she had talked with Dad that very morning. We long knew that finding Dad alone on the front porch at five o'clock in the morning made for a perfect time for talking to him. This was when you might get him to agree to something you wanted, or maybe even negotiate some sort of reprieve from being grounded. That meant that my sleepy-head sister had been up early. I was impressed!

She said they had talked and he listened while she told him why she was protesting. After a while, they agreed to terms for her to continue with the rallies. Things like he had to know when, where, and how long she would be gone. He announced, and she had to concede, that if he had to pick her up from the back of a police car again, her protests were over. Despite that, she told me, "I stood my ground." She told Dad she had never thrown a bottle or seen anyone else throw one.

Dad believed Deb, but said to watch out anyway, because they might be setting up the protesters to bring a halt to the marches. He warned, "Besides, you never know when I'll just come by and watch from a distance." She acknowledged that, saying, "I'll agree to that, but what about Claudette?" Dad looked over his glasses as he instructed, "Take her every now and then, just not often. But watch over her. For God's sake, I may tolerate your why, but don't tell your mother! She'd throw a fit!"

Deb and I were drinking Faygo Redpop at the back door of the house when she told me about her conversation with Dad. She also told me that I could go to a rally over the weekend, "But you have to stay close to me!" I grinned.

She had one arm around my shoulder while the other held a bottle of soda. She took the thumb of her hand holding the pop bottle and wiped the Redpop moustache off my face. "Real close. I mean it." I smiled, "I promise!"

That Saturday, the sun was shining bright and there was a breeze in the air. Dressed in my finest bell bottom jeans, I picketed, carrying the "Make Love, Not War," sign. It was my favorite of all the signs we'd made. I'd made another copy for our bedroom wall, along with one that read, "Help Save Water, Shower With Steady." However, that one was just for our bedroom, it certainly wasn't for public consumption.

Lifting the stick so my sign was high in the air, I proudly walked in circles around the local courthouse with my big sister and maybe a hundred other people. I think Deb picked this rally for me because it would be safer for me in our local town.

Suddenly, amidst the loud crowd, the voice of one boy rang out. Wearing a bright red hoodie, he was sprinting at full speed. Not even turning to the person he thought he was talking to, the boy called out, "Turn left – I think we lost 'em." Deb tumbled and nearly fell over the boy as he was crossing in the middle of the protesters and bumped into her.

I grabbed her sign for extra support at the last minute, preventing her fall. The boy in the red hoodie was Johnny. He had fallen to the ground at a forty-five-degree angle smack dab in front of Deb.

He was almost up and back to a start position, ready to take off again from the ground. I could tell he recognized Deb's voice as she was yelling, "What the fuck, Johnny!" I could see the recognition in his face. He was back up and in his running position, but he turned his head back as he said, "Sorry, Deb!" Then he took off again, racing like a bolt of lightning while he flashed the peace sign!

About two minutes later, we saw Billy. He was weaving in and out of the crowd, headed in the same direction as Johnny. He had wings on his feet, too. I wondered what in the world they were up to. We would all hear the whole story a few days later.

CHAPTER TEN

Early one evening, a group of us were gathered at the shack. We were seated on the logs and rocks outside. We were seated on the logs and rocks outside. Johnny, Gate, Nancy, Deb, Ronnie, Billy, Sharon, Sandy, and Kari were all there, smoking and talking, as even more kids were coming to the area.

Billy decided to tell the whole story of the incident at the rally, "I'll tell you what happened on the day of the march!" Johnny wasn't happy, "Fuck, no!" Billy had a chance at his moment of glory. Nothing, including all of Johnny's protests, would stop him from obtaining his fifteen minutes of fame.

Johnny and Billy had started their day by breaking into an empty Beach cottage, only to be caught in the act by the homeowner. Chris Powers, the homeowner, was a man of about sixty and a friend of my dad's. He'd chased the boys on his four-wheeler throughout the Beach that morning, determined to catch them this time. It wasn't his first rodeo with his house being burglarized.

Finally, in a last-ditch attempt to get away from their very aggravated and persistent pursuer, the desperate boys headed to the highway. They hitched a ride to town as a last resort; after running from Chris's dogged pursuit for two hours, they couldn't think of another way to escape. Unbeknownst to Billy, it was the last place in the whole world that Johnny wanted to go.

Kyle Stein, a druggie from town, was driving past the Beach on Old North Dixie Highway as the boys raced toward the road with their thumbs out. Figuring they might have some weed, he stopped and picked them up. He was right – they did, so they all smoked a couple of joints before Kyle dropped them off near the protest. That was when Johnny confessed to Billy. Their trouble was worse in town than it was with Chris Powers.

Right after Kyle left, Johnny spilled the beans to Billy about going into town. It turned out that Johnny had made a drug deal with a guy named Greg Van Marshall, a twenty-year-old, and a gang of boys from town. Johnny hadn't told Billy anything about it until that very moment. Johnny's big concern was that he had bought the drugs on credit and hadn't been able to pay the drug dealers. Johnny

125

knew they were after him. Because this was the first that Billy found out Johnny had made a deal without cutting him in, Billy was pissed. Johnny told Billy, "I haven't been able to turn it over. I was going to cut you in after I sold it. It was a surprise."

Billy didn't believe a single word of what Johnny said. A fight ensued between them. Johnny pushed Billy down a nearby hill, and then he took off running. A pissed off Billy got back on his feet and pursued Johnny down the slope and into the crowded courthouse area.

Johnny was much faster and way ahead of Billy. However, the endless flash of the red hoodie in the crowd gave Billy hope, so he continued chasing after Johnny. When Johhny fell into Deb, Billy was able to gain ground on him. But when Billy was finally able to catch up to Johnny, it was too late.

His buddy had collapsed against a wall in an alley. Johnny had been stabbed by the drug dealers, who had also spotted him in the crowd as he was running from Billy. They cornered Johnny, slashed him good and took off.

Just a minute or so behind, Billy found Johnny alone, holding his bleeding arm. Billy helped Johnny up, got him back to the Beach, and patched up his arm. Johnny wasn't hurt too badly, because he was walking around the neighborhood and talking to everybody the very next day.

Billy said, "Pretty stupid of Johnny to wear a red hoodie for a B&E. No one could miss finding him on the Beach. But he was even easier to spot at the rally downtown. That's when Greg and his goons picked up my chase! Everywhere I looked, I could see that red hoodie in that crowd of marchers. Greg managed to catch up to him before I could!" Everyone was laughing as a giggling Nancy said, "A red hoodie! That's dumb, Johnny!"

"He was bleeding like a broken water pipe when I found him!" Of course, Billy wanted to go back and show everyone the blood in the alley, but as we pointed out to him, that could only happen after Johnny paid the dealers what he owed them.

Johnny didn't like being called dumb or showing any kind of weakness. He was pissed that Billy told the story in a way to make himself the hero! The look on Johnny's face was one of rage. It was just past dark when Billy finished the story. The street lights were on and Hank came looking for Deb and me. Deb and I turned around when we heard, "Deb, Claudette – you over there?"

"Yes, Hank – we're on our way." Johnny, still mad over being call dumb, lashed out at Hank with one of his racial tirades ending with the statement to Hank, "I'll fuck you up!"

Deb and I headed for Hank. But by that point, she was resolutely walking toward the shack. Hank was carrying a black baseball bat, "The only thing blacker than me is this bat, Johnny!" Everyone went silent, especially Johnny, who cringed as Hank approached. Deb and I knew Hank could take care of herself with Johnny or anybody else. The three of us walked away together, without hearing a peep from Johnny or any of the others.

The next day, my dad talked to Chris, who was still pissed about the break-in. Chris was talking about calling the police on Johnny and Billy. However, with a little persuasion from Dad, Chris agreed to give the boys just one more chance. Hours later, Dad saw Billy and Johnny coming up the street near the garage.

He called them over, "You boys gotta stop breaking into people's houses. Chris is pissed – rightfully so. That's his property!" Johnny responded, "Yeah, yeah." Dad looked over his glasses, "You got until five o'clock today to go by and apologize or he's calling the cops. That's all the time I could buy you!"

Johnny replied, "No fucking way!" Billy, this time the smarter of the two, disagreed, "Johnny! Yes, we'll do that, Mr. Mack. Even if Johnny doesn't, I will – I don't wanna go to jail!" Billy pulled Johnny away. The two grumbled and argued as they headed up the street. It turned out that they both apologized to Chris. Dad would try to save as many of the kids as he could. Of course, there were some who were determined not to heed sage advice.

Our summer was moving forward. Mom and Dad were excited to have off the same Saturday night, so they decided to go dancing. Mom was dressed up in a black tea-length gown. Dad was looking fine in an all-black suit and fedora. The kids watched as the parents walked into the local clubhouse party. It was adults only that night, or so they thought. We planned to eavesdrop through the windows as a start to our evening.

We'd been watching and interfering with the set-up people all afternoon. Mike snagged two bottles of wine while the workers were being distracted by the kids. We knew what band was playing. Their name was written on the drums, "The Real Beach Boys." As night came, we were watching from the breakwall; all the parents inside were having a party. And there was us, peeking through the open windows. I always wondered if they knew we were there.

We snuck up closer and closer to the window. I could hear Mom and Dad talking to a lady called Shelly. She had a daughter named Jolie. Jolie was a little older than us; I didn't know her at all. According to their conversation, Jolie had been sent to a hospital or something to stop her from using heroin. Jolie's dad left them after it happened.

I knew what heroin was – kind of – from books and Dad. Dad told me it was really dangerous, could hook you, kill you, or leave you crazy, something like that. He said the addicts injected it with needles into their arms – that ruled it out for me. Just like Nancy said, he warned us they could lace cigarettes and pot to make someone dependent on the drug.

Nancy was peering in the window next to me and told me she knew Jolie. I was surprised and hurt, "How come I don't? You're my best friend!" Nancy smiled, "Always – that's why I never introduced you. You wouldn't like her – I didn't take to her, either. I don't know her well or anything." I accepted that answer, and through the window we watched as Mom and Dad danced to the "Tennessee Waltz."

Then we kids headed down to the lake, with Nancy and me on my motorcycle and the others walking. News had come from Mike that the girl found murdered at the lake was named Megan Regan. He heard that she was from San Francisco. That gave us something to talk about. Nancy got off and lit a cigarette. I stayed seated across my motorcycle, talking.

Mike quickly popped out with, "Seems like Deb knew this Megan girl." I was furious! "No, she could have been to one of the rallies, but I've been to them – there are hundreds of people. I asked Deb, she said she might have seen her there, but doesn't know her at all. Stop your lying!"

Joey came in with a chuckle, "Yeah, like knowing some stranger you see at a football stadium!" Then he turned to me with, "But, that's bullshit about the protests; you've never been to any." I was proud and showed it. I told

him, "Have too! I even make signs for them!"
Nancy jumped in to defend me, "Yep, it's true.
I've helped her, too!"

Johnny seemed to know more, 'It's true.
Last week there were marches. Deb was there,
cops were involved and I saw her outrun 'em."
I quickly told him, "No way!" Johnny went on
to say, "Well, that sure was a cop chasing her
and Ronnie!" Johnny passed me a joint, but I
waved him off, "Later." I just left all of them
there. I wanted to be alone.

But after a minute, I decided to head
straight home to ask Deb. Alas, it was true!
Deb had been in trouble again at a rally. Why
was I always the last to know? Deb told me it
happened a lot at the protests, but Dad didn't
know about it.

It was well after midnight that Saturday
night when Deb and I finally saw Mom and
Dad again. We watched them come walking
up the sidewalk to the house after the party.
They stopped, looked up, and saw the light on
in our bedroom window. Then they smiled
slyly before they hugged and kissed near the
house. You could always see the longing in
my parent's love and their need for each
other's embraces.

That night, Nancy sneaked in the house long after all of us were asleep. Early the next morning, Nancy and I heard Deb and Dad talking on the porch. "Honestly, I may have seen Megan, but I didn't know her. Dad, people come from all over to these marches." Dad gently smiled, "I know, baby. That's what worries me." Deb responded, "Dad, it seems she was killed by somebody and then put into the lake. At least, that's what I've heard the cops are thinking. That probably means the killer was some transient or contractor from some factory up north of here, not a local."

Dad looked over the top of his glasses at Deb, "That girl had needle marks in her arms." Deb looked Dad straight in the eyes, "I don't drink and I don't do drugs. I'm only marching for a better world!" Dad smiled, "I know Deb; you're too smart for any of that." Deb was telling him the absolute truth. She wasn't interested in either.

Although I did see her drunk – and it was just a week later. It happened on a Friday. Deb was really mad at Dad because he wouldn't let her go to a march in Cleveland on the next day, a Saturday. He was adamant. Mom had the whole weekend off and wanted us to spend time as a family. They had already made plans for all of us to take a trip to Boblo Island that very same Saturday.

Deb came up to our room in a fury. She was lugging a big straw-wrapped bottle of Chianti, what they call a fiasco, she had nabbed from our parent's liquor cabinet. Pissed off, she called Ronnie to pick us up. She carried the wine bottle in a tote bag. In the car, in the middle of her rants about Cleveland, she started drinking straight from the bottle.

Before long, we were in town walking around with Ronnie. Ronnie and I were trying to stop Deb from drinking. By dark, she was practically dead drunk, sitting on a curb beside Front Street. Her fiasco of Chianti became quite the fiasco for her! She was quite a sight – drunk as a skunk and throwing up.

We finally managed to get her back in the car and home. Thankfully for Deb, Mom and Dad had already left for work. It took both of us to get her out of the car and upstairs. Once we got her safely in bed, she promptly passed out. Ronnie and I went downstairs to listen to music and laugh at her antics of the evening. Before he left, I slipped upstairs so I could give him protest signs for the group going to Cleveland. Naturally, Deb was out cold. She

134

didn't even stir when I made a bunch of noise by accidentally dropping signs on the floor.

Of course, she woke the next morning with a crushing wine hangover and threw up a little more. However, her fate was sealed. She was going to Boblo Island; there was no way for her to get out of it. She also understood the need to hide her hangover from our parents. She knew the hardest part would be the boat ride to the island.

Not surprisingly, during the boat ride to the island, Deb was throwing up over the side. Dad caught on pretty fast, asking, "Deb, you okay?" She looked up at him, as she donned her dark sunglasses and said, "I was pissed over Cleveland, and so I got pissed on Mom's bottle of Chianti!" Deb wasn't much for lying and she'd stand her ground.

Dad laughed, "This'll teach you. Have a great boat ride, missy! For me, you'll do you penitence here. However, I suggest you keep all of this from your mom. Hell's fury is nothing compared to your mother if she gets wind of this one!" Then grinning widely, he continued, "She'll ground you for life – or maybe even longer." Deb, looking a little green, weakly nodded.

Throughout the day, Deb wore her dark sunglasses while she was popping aspirin like candy, all the while trying to find quiet places to sit on the island. Dad made sure that she didn't have an instant's peace. Whether it was a jovial slap on the back, a loud voice in her ear, or a big plate of greasy fries, he was making sure she felt every single moment of her hangover!

I think the best part of that trip to Boblo was watching the two of them spar, father to hungover daughter and her right back at him, all with a marvelous sense of humor. She was taking all the medicine Dad was dishing out and tossing a few protest slogans back at him like, "We Shall Overcome." Deb turned out to be a lifelong nondrinker, except for one or two single-malt whiskies on a trip to Ireland many years later.

Now, back to our story. Dad and Deb could engage in debates, and on the porch that long-ago summer morning, the discussion about the dead girl on the beach continued, "Dad, this girl probably didn't know anyone in this area. I'm always with Ronnie and a group of people I know well." Dad just looked to Deb, "Just watch out, baby. And you know, call me if you need me. No matter what it is."

Late that evening, riding my motorcycle just before the street lights came on, I saw Dad, Deb, and Peaches headed toward the shack where I had been hanging out. Dad pointed to the street light and it came on as though he had just ordered it to shine. I immediately stopped, and then we all laughed. "See, I was really close to being on time, for once!" Dad just shook his head with a grin as they all turned and followed me home.

Dad came into the garage and told me, "I don't want you at that shack, it's caving in and has rusty nails. I'm reworking the green house and the lot next door came with it. You can play there after this week. It's safer." I nodded and said, "Okay." I knew I had better agree with Dad about this – it wasn't something he would be willing to compromise about. I wasn't entirely sure I'd never go back to our shack, but I'd try to spend less time there – or at least avoid getting caught again. But I'm sure I would be told about it many more times … I smiled and walked into the house with Dad and Peaches.

The following day, I decided to stop by the house of parties where we had skipped school. During the summer, I really didn't expect much to be going on. But Johnny and

Billy were on the porch when I pulled up, "Hey. Nancy here?" From the smirks on their faces, I should've seen something coming. "Yeah, come on in!" I parked the bike and went in. Johnny and Billy followed me inside, quietly giggling. I figured the boys were up to something, but they always were, so I ignored all the signs. Gate, Kim, Joey, Mike, Sandy, Sharon, and Kari were all in the living room. "Where's Nancy?" I asked.

Just then, Johnny tossed a towel to me, "She's out back. Here, they need a towel in that room." There was a closed door to my left. Without even thinking, I opened it and started to take the towel inside. Within seconds I was stopped in my tracks.

On the bed were Barbara and Freddie! He had his pants pulled partway down and she only had socks on. I tossed the towel out of pure reflex. As it landed on the floor, Freddie turned to see me as I closed the door.

Everybody in the living room was roaring with laughter. Just then, I heard Nancy, "You son of a bitches!" She grabbed me by the hand and took me outside, "Those assholes! I'm so sorry, Claudette. I know you really have a thing for Freddie."

I looked at her, "I just want to go!" Then I got on my motorcycle and left. I drove to the ballpark where I sat, hidden and crying. I was crushed. I thought of all the things Freddie had said to me on our morning beach walks. Like how I was special, the kind of girl a boy marries one day. I was heartbroken. After a while, I just got on my bike and headed home.

As soon as I entered the house, I raced upstairs to our bedroom. I really needed to talk with Deb about what had just happened. She would understand and maybe help me with what I was feeling. Instead, I found Ronnie and Deb in bed naked together with the covers over them. Deb's voice rang out in shock, "Get out!" I raced down the stairs, flopped on the couch, put a pillow over my head and screamed with all my might!

A few minutes later the phone rang. When I picked it up, it was Barbara hollering, "He's mine now! Stay away, bitch!" In a moment of pure and absolute clarity I shouted, "Barbara, fuck you!" Then I slammed the phone down.

CHAPTER ELEVEN

That summer, I would begin to get some answers about Civil Rights, and not from books or the news.

The high school in town had an open house, introducing new students to the school and welcoming back the upperclassmen for the upcoming September. Deb and I decided to go, just for fun. Neither of us had ever been inside that school.

After all, among the hundreds who would be attending the open house at the school, probably no one would have any idea that we were Beach kids. Ronnie gave us a ride into town, dropping us off shortly before the opening at nine o'clock in the morning.

There were a lot of people in the front of the high school, so Ronnie dropped us off on Willow Street, near the entrance at the back of the building. We saw a sign on the door that read, "Open House – Enter in Front." We went in the back door anyway, and then made our way through the empty hall toward the front of the school.

It wasn't long before we slipped into an empty classroom at the end of the hall, instead of turning the corner and walking down an intersecting hallway toward the front door of the building. Once we were in the classroom, we peered out a window to see what was going on at the front of the building. We saw the crowds outside had signs and were screaming slogans, too. The White people carried signs that read, "We Want White Tenants in Our Communities" "No Blacks" "White School." Then we saw a bus pulling up with signs on its sides that read, "Soul People, Nothing But Soul," "Human Rights," and "Civil Rights."

As we came out of the classroom, we quietly worked our way further down the empty hallway toward the main entrance of the school. Just past the front doors, the hall near the gymnasium was packed with high school boys. A man who appeared to be a school coach was giving out baseball bats to the White teenaged boys. As they got bats, they were lining up along the interior walls all the way to the front entrance, brandishing their weapons. We could hear racist words being uttered. It was a damn Mexican standoff.

Deb could see the writing on the wall and grabbed my hand, "Come on! This is no time to be here." We retreated back to the exit where we had entered. However, that door had been locked and chained.

Deb and I raced to a phone in an empty teachers' lounge nearby. She called Dad – no answer, "He must be at the green house." She dialed fast, Dad answered, and she told him where we were and what was happening, "Don't try to get out, stay hidden. Look through a window for me walking up, then run out the front door. I'm on my way."

What happened next became a legend in our unassuming little town. Mr. Pines was with Dad when the call came and he insisted on going along and driving, saying, "We're better together, Mack. I got the wheel." Dad told Mr. Pines, "I need to go into the house for a second. I think I better grab Old Salty." Mr. Pines followed Dad into the house, "I'm coming too. I'm just making sure I'm your lawyer all the way."

Dad silently opened the hall closet door, entered, then took a long coat from a hook on the wall of the staircase. Behind the coat was a hidden door leading to a room under the large stairwell. Dad opened the door; inside the room under the stairs was his gun safe. He opened the safe and took out a forty-five revolver and Old Salty, a sawed-off shotgun.

Putting the forty-five in the waist of his jeans, he laid his long wool coat over his arm to hide both the sawed-off shotgun and the handgun. As soon as he saw exactly what Dad was doing, Mr. Pines started walking toward the front door as he told Dad, "I'll start the car." Then he headed to the waiting car and opened up the passenger door, before getting into the car behind the steering wheel and starting the engine.

Dad followed him a few seconds later, heading down the sidewalk to Mr. Pines and the idling car. Getting inside, Dad tossed the coat in the back seat and placed his forty-five in the glove box, below some papers and candy bars. As he closed the glove box door, he told Mr. Pines, "This one's for you." Mr. Pines smiled. "I have one under my seat." They took off in a hurry, heading to town.

Mr. Pines drove like a bat out of hell to the high school. We estimated the elapsed time at fifteen minutes from Deb's phone call until we saw Dad step out of the passenger seat of Mr. Pines's car. The sleeves on Dad's blue work shirt were still rolled up from working and his long, tanned arm was holding the shotgun straight down by his side. He started a slow, stone-cold walk toward the crowd. Mr. Pines turned the four door Cadillac sedan around and parked it in a getaway position, its engine still running.

We could see Dad approaching the crowd in the distance. We didn't move until we saw him move his gun enough for the onlookers to see its barrel. As soon as they did, the crowd split as though Moses had just entered the arena. Deb and I hauled ass down that hall to the front, headed for the entrance. Dad strode up those steps, eyes glued to the ground.

I called out to the coach, "That's my dad coming for us! Better open that door!" The coach was terrified by the approach of a towering armed man, who looked only at the ground. He opened the door for Dad, and stood to the side with the boys as the door closed behind Dad. He looked up at us, "Let's go! Move it!"

As we turned to leave with Dad, he saw a Black girl. She was maybe thirteen, hiding and crying in a nook near the exit. He paused,

"Deb, get her!" Deb stopped, stretched out her hand, and the girl came willingly. When Dad was ready for the coach to open the door again, he said to us, "Behind me, single file, and don't even think about stopping."

Then Dad looked at the coach, motioned with a slight lift of the gun barrel, and nodded. When he did that, the nervous coach opened the door for us. We left the same way Dad came, as the stone-cold, quiet crowd parted like the Red Sea.

Mr. Pines had every single door open on that Cadillac. We were all in the car and out of there in seconds. After he got on the road, he looked in the back seat, "Polly!" Polly, the young Black girl who had been crying, suddenly stopped, "Mr. Pines!"

My dad smiled at Mr. Pines, "You know this little one?" Mr. Pines nodded, "Sure do, that's Polly Taylor! You're all right, baby. Are you staying at your grandpa JoJo's house?" Polly sniffling, quietly said, "Yes, Mr. Pines. Mom and Dad are at work." She looked at his eyes in the rear-view mirror as Mr. Pines comforted her, "No problem, we'll take you to him." Then he looked to Dad, "We're heading across the tracks to the East Side."

In a low voice, Dad told Mr. Pines, "On the way, stop the car on the Winchester Street Bridge." Mr. Pines nodded. Dad was watching out the windows as the car approached the bridge. Once we were near the middle of the bridge he said, "Stop here. No one's around." Mr. Pines pulled over close to the rail.

Dad took the sawed-off gun, tossed it out the car window so hard it sailed over the railing of the bridge and far into the Rasin River. Mr. Pines grinned, "No state in the Union where that gun's legal. Sorry about that Mack – it was a nice piece."

Dad smiled ruefully at Mr. Pines, "Well, it's gone now. I made that one, I can make another – after I see if this day brings trouble. Everything else I have is legal. Actually, that one lasted a long time. I made it in the South, for riding shotgun with my Uncle Claude on some of his adventures. He was famous for the cars he souped up for running moonshine, and for driving them for just that purpose. Like you – a hell of a driver!" Both men laughed.

We headed on to the east side of town, where Polly's grandfather JoJo lived. Mr. Pines and Polly got out of the car, "Be right back." Mr. Pines walked Polly through a yard and up to the house. He called out as he opened the screen door, "JoJo, it's Pines. I brought Polly home." Polly ran inside as JoJo Taylor came to the door. Mr. Pines went in and stayed for a few minutes.

Deb smiled at Dad, "See, I can judge the temperature at these marches. This one looked like it could get out of control fast – especially with the coach handing out those bats." Dad smiled, "Smart cookie. It sure did look like it was going downhill fast."

Dad, being Dad, turned to both of us in the back seat, "Hey, Pines usually has some candy in the glove box. I believe we should check!" Dad knew these were upsetting events for us, what with his shotgun out and all. So, he was looking to calm his girls down. Nosing around in Mr. Pines's glove box was his best solution and it made us all laugh.

We were all eating Payday candy bars as we saw Mr. Pines coming out of the house, walking toward the car. Polly and her grandpa stayed on the porch and waived. The old man looked at my father in the passenger seat and nodded his head to him. Dad nodded back at him. As Mr. Pines pulled away, he told my dad, "Mr. Taylor wanted me to thank you for

147

saving his granddaughter and said to tell you that if you ever need anything at all, you just need to ask him."

I want to tell you about the long wool trench coat my dad used to cover the shotgun as he walked the thirty steps down our front sidewalk and to the car. Because it was summer when Deb and I so untimely decided to visit the town school at the beginning of the race riots, you, our reader, were deprived an understanding of the full value of that coat. That simply will not do!

It was about six years earlier – Christmas time of 1961. I was about nine years old. That's when I got my first inkling of how special Dad's coat really was. Mom took Deb and me to Toledo to pick up a gift she had ordered for Dad. We arrived at a place with a sign on the door that read, "The Tailor Shop."

After we went inside, the owner brought out two matching long coats. I recognized one of them as my father's trench coat because of the moth holes in the black wool. Mom had been really upset when she saw the damage to the coat that autumn. When she showed him, Dad reassured her, "Now Ruby, you know that coat's perfectly serviceable, and those holes are so itty-bitty – no one will ever even notice any of them at all."

The second coat was brand new, but it looked identical, except there were no moth holes in it. My mother asked the man, "Now, you're sure those inside pockets are an exact match to the old coat?" He told her the entire coat was an exact copy of the old one, just brand new. He emphatically told her that he had double-checked and triple-checked every last measurement when he made it. Mom examined it very closely, and then finally announced that she was satisfied.

On Christmas night, Dad was surprised by Mom's gift of the coat. I saw him trying it on for Mom. They were inside that large walk-in closet beside the stairs. It was the very same closet that held the hook for his coat just over the panel door in the staircase wall. His gun safe was open behind the door.

Dad took his sawed-off gun, the one he later threw to the bottom of the Rasin River, and slipped it into the right inside pocket of his new coat. That inside pocket had a hole in the bottom of it, but the pocket was too small for the trigger guard of the gun to fit into it. Basically, that pocket was a sleeve that held the barrel of the gun. Then Dad put his hand in the right pocket on the outside of the coat. The outside pocket had a flap that he could put his hand through and he did just that, taking ahold of the handle of the gun inside the coat.

Then he moved the shotgun slightly out from under the coat with precise control of it. Back and forth, inside outside, a few inches up and down, clearly playing with Mom. "Ruby, I love it. It's a perfect fit." My mother winked, "Now, put that damn thing away!"

So now, going back to 1967 – on a day shortly after the incident at the school, Dad was working outside the green house. I was playing in the back yard, when Mr. Pines arrived with a wave as he approached Dad in the yard. Within only a few minutes, I heard them deep in conversation.

Dad told Mr. Pines, "I'm positive about it now. Like I told you before, I really do regret buying this house. I'm worried about Deb and Claudette – especially after that dead girl in the lake. As you know, drugs are just pouring into this area!" Pines nodded, "I understand."

My dad went on to tell him, "I was out patrolling with some of the guys. We found a security contractor just randomly walking around in the community yesterday. He said he worked for the Stoker Plant. After we talked with him for a minute or two, he asked if any Blacks lived in the area." We ran him out with this stern warning, "Next time you come here my Mrs. Forty-Five will greet your ass. Then we followed him to the exit. He got into a car with Ohio plates. I don't like any of this nonsense going on around the girls."

Mr. Pines looked concerned as he told Dad, "I told you last week that this was coming. It's the beginning of a spillover that's coming down from the Civil Rights movement in Detroit. Your guy yesterday was probably scouting out whether this was a good place to make a stand against the Blacks from Detroit. We saw what happened at the school last week. There's more coming! There are groups looking to cause trouble on both sides. But this is a fight for Civil Rights, Mack. It's not going to fade away." Dad looked solemnly at Mr. Pines, "I hear you."

Then Dad's face changed, "Son of a bitch! You sure that it's coming?" Mr. Pines did not hesitate, "Mack, it's coming this way, maybe tonight, two days, tops. That's why I'm here. I was in Detroit yesterday. It's White on

Black, Black on White up there now. Mostly words, but this is going to escalate! I'm worried about both our families. I won't be going back for a few days. They'll need me when it's over, if I'm right."

Dad patted Mr. Pines on the left shoulder, "You're the smartest man I know. Walk with me." The two men walked over to the side of the house, and from there, into the lot to talk. I could no longer hear what they were saying, but I knew something serious was going on. The men talked for about fifteen minutes. Then Mr. Pines waved goodbye to me as he was leaving.

Dad told me to come on. Then he locked up the green house and we headed home across the street. I really didn't even ask what was going on. That just wasn't like the usual inquisitive me, but I think I was still absorbing what I just heard. Dad sat on the porch and told me to, "Run inside – and then send your sister out to talk with me."

Alone, Deb and Dad walked in the yard and talked. However, the events that unfolded over the next forty-eight hours taught me so much about what was really going on in this not always perfect world.

CHAPTER TWELVE

There was an old friend of Dad's in the neighborhood they called JD, a really nice guy. He only had one lung – for some reason, I remember that. Anyway, he came over. The men went off to do some major food shopping, all alone. It was strange because we'd usually ride along. But that time, Dad said no to me, adding, "Your sister will tell you everything about what's happening."

After they left, Deb told me Mom was on her way home early. She added, "We're going to have a whole lot of people coming here for a day or two, Ette. We're all going to have to stay in the house, yard and garage. Seems like the Civil Rights marches in Detroit are turning into riots. They're small now, but escalating. Dad and Mr. Pines are afraid they'll be moving down to this area. White supremacists have been scouting our Beach looking to find out if Blacks live here. We're located right in the middle of a mess, ground zero for a massive collision of stuff rolling down from Detroit and up from Toledo."

That was when I realized something major was coming, but surprisingly, I wasn't afraid. A little while later, Dad, JD, Deb, and I unloaded groceries from Dad's car. The back seat was stuffed to overflowing and the trunk was packed full of food, too. Carrying it all inside took us a whole lot of trips. Once everything was in the house, we managed to put it all away. It was far more than any normal shopping trip.

Later that afternoon, the four of us were in the garage, hanging black cloth on the side windows to block anyone outside from seeing in. Just then, Mom pulled into the driveway. She saw us and got out of the car in an angry fit, "What the hell are you doing hanging those black drapes? I told ya, if you ever made another drop of moonshine …"

Dad interrupted, "Ruby – stop! I told you to come home 'cause we've got lots of trouble brewing!" Then he quickly walked over to the car and had a quiet conversation with my mom. She promptly said, "Oh, let's get ready then. I'll call Claire and Lara – and Dale better close the bar and come." Dad just looked worried, "Whoever you think, but get them here fast. Food's in and cars can park in the lot across the street."

Lara and Dale were lifelong friends of my parents and they owned a small bar in town. Lara, a tall lovely blonde about forty-five, was from Germany, and then she had lived in London through WWII. That's where she met and married Dale, a soldier stationed there during the war.

Over the next hours, people congregated at our home. Hank, Claire, the twins, Lara, Dale, Mr. Pines, his wife, kids, and many other families all showed up. There were also a few buddies of Dad – Charlie, JR, Mr. Bornstein, and others, some with their wives and kids. All told, there were more than forty people filling our little cottage, yard, and garage.

Everyone was bringing something – food, blankets, flashlights, radios, and more. Mom and Lara stacked blankets and pillows around the walls of the large main living area, the glassed-in foyer, their bedroom, our bedroom, and put extras in the garage. Everyone would have a place to lay their head.

Dad and JD had stocked the refrigerators in the house and the garage with perishables; everything else that wouldn't fit in the kitchen went to our big bedroom and the garage. The pantries were full, counters were overflowing with snacks, and coolers full of ice held soda pop. We were told to play with the kids only in the fenced yard between our house and garage. Mom told us, "Later, all the kids will sleep in your room – so be sure to make them as comfortable as you can."

Dad told me to tell Nancy or any of the other kids we knew that they were welcome, but if they came onto our property, they would stay until it was over. He said he couldn't be opening the property to let people in and out. But he told us that the Beach entrances were also being secured by other men.

I called Nancy, who was at home. She was still asleep after a late night. I told her what was happening. She came by a little later, but chose not to stay, "Fuck, I'm not gonna be locked down." I told her it was her choice, "But if you decide to come back, you know Dad will let you in, no matter when." She cheerfully said, "Yeah."

"I don't want Johnny here at all. Tell the others, except Johnny, everybody has to obey the rules – except that they get just one entry here – before dark. Once they're in, there's no going back out. Also, let them know if they don't want to come here, the front entrance gates to the Beach will be guarded by a bunch of the men, so some of the boys could go there if they want to help. After all, there are three entrances to cover!" Nancy gave me a big hug and took off across the field, and then headed up the next street.

That evening, the street lights on our road somehow felt dimmer. It was weird. Every single thing outside the property appeared extra quiet. Summer nights always produced boys playing after dark, but not that night. My guess was they either went to help the men at the Beach entrances or locked their souls down in some local drug house.

Mom kept reassuring us that we had nothing to worry about, because all of the men would be sitting guard on the front and back of the house. I think she was quite nervous and the presence of all the people was taking a toll. Mom was not a hostess kind of mother. But for those nights, she went the extra mile for everyone staying on the property.

Even when they told us other men would be guarding all the Beach entrances after dark, I wasn't fazed. I trusted my dad to take care of whatever would come. Why this did not scare me, or at least seem abnormal, I don't know.

Everyone was watching TV, talking, or listening to news on radios. Kids were playing board games and more in my room. Mom noticed that Lara was getting pretty upset at the news, so Mom took her into the kitchen for a talk, "Lara, I know what you're thinking. This isn't London. We'll all be fine." Mom reached out for her and Lara held onto Mom as they hugged.

Then she poured Lara a drink and they sat down at the kitchen table. A couple of other women joined them. When they saw Lara was so teary-eyed, they asked if she was okay. Mom quickly jumped in with, "She's fine. Lara, you don't have to talk about it."

Lara looked at Mom, "I survived it, so I surely can talk about it." Ruby smiled as Lara told the others at the table, "During the war, I was stuck under rubble of a building in London for three days. Dale's the soldier who found me and pulled me out." Mom jumped in to lighten the mood, "Now that's a hell of a love story!" Everyone laughed, even Lara began to giggle, despite her blushing face, and the mood lightened quickly.

Mr. Pines had foreseen the onrushing bad times correctly. In the early morning hours of

July 23, 1967, the police raided an after-hours blind pig – that's what they used to call unlicensed bars for Black patrons – on the West Side of Detroit.

These establishments had flourished (in part, by paying off police to avoid being raided) since the turn of the twentieth century and right through Prohibition. There were blind pigs in Detroit, New York and just about every city around the country. In those times of segregation, they provided entertainment for the Black middle-class and were their only alternative to trying to go to the White-owned bars that would not allow them to enter, much less serve them.

During the raid of the blind pig that night, the cops arrested several people. The bar had been hosting a big party to celebrate three local Black soldiers returning from Vietnam. In response to the raid and the arrests, a group of people outside the bar got angry. A bottle was thrown at a police car. The policemen reacted with anger.

That started the ball rolling. By eight in the morning, crowds numbering in the thousands had already formed on the streets. Police completely lost control of the civil rights protesters in the area around Clairmont Street; the race riots had begun.

There were fist fights, stabbings, police officers shooting into crowds, glass breaking, tear gas, looting, tanks rolling through the streets, and to quote Mr. Pines, "Detroit was being burnt to the ground." For the next forty-eight hours, our house was filled with people – most all of them paying attention to the nonstop news coverage from Detroit on the TVs and radios.

Two men were on the front porch of our home and two more were in the garage with the large door open. All were seated with radios, small TVs, and walkie-talkies. The men sat guard in shifts. Iced tea, coffee, and food were brought to them mostly by Mom, Claire, and Hank. But I think everyone kept checking on the men, with offerings of food or coffee. They were all well cared for.

Oh, I forgot to mention – the men sat in teams of two, one Black man with one White man, each with a loaded shotgun hidden below baby blankets. Every single man would watch a different direction down the road, both in front and at the back of our home and garage. At the Beach entrances, men with lawn chairs filled the grounds, every one with a shotgun on display for all to see.

While all of those men were guarding the entrances to the private beach community, they turned away two unknown vehicles at gunpoint. Each car had Ohio plates and held a number of unknown White men inside. Dad would tell me later that he was sure the man they had chased out of the Beach a day or two earlier was a racist scout.

Although it was deemed safe for people to leave our home after two days, the rioting in Detroit continued for five. We'd hear of events that had taken place in our town, fighting between Black and White kids. The fights seem to have happened near a bowling alley. Police broke those up.

On the connecting roads between town and the Beaches, an older boy, maybe twenty, was dragged behind a car. We had no idea who the boy dragged was. We heard it both ways, some said the boy dragged was White and the boys in the car were Black – but for others, he was Black, and the car's occupants were White. We never did know the truth, but it sounded like someone really was dragged behind a car during the violence.

161

In later years, my father told me the logic behind barricading us all inside one house – our house. Mr. Pines and Dad had figured no matter who came rioting, whether Black or White, that the one of them who was the same race might be able to steer the bad guys away from the property. We were really very lucky, looking back; the uproar and violence stayed mostly in Detroit. I also think by the time these forty-eight hours had passed; I had grown up some. For the first time in my life, I saw the world as something much more immense than the sphere of my easy, insular existence.

In the days that would follow, my dad always seemed worried when he heard Mr. Pines was making a trip to Detroit. Mr. Pines worked as a lawyer with an organization that helped release jailed civil rights protesters. He'd get a phone call and head up to bail some people out of jail, usually on a moment's notice. That seem to be his main duty at that time – while trying to keep himself and his family alive and safe.

Dad and Mr. Pines had been friends since before Dad married my mom. They had a long history together. Mr. Pines was a customer in Dale's bar in the 1950s, it was one of the few non-segregated bars for miles around.

Mom worked for Lara and Dale while she was waiting to get a job at a Ford factory. One evening, she wasn't putting up with the rude remarks from a guy in the bar. After all, she could hold her own. But when the guy slapped her ass as she walked away from his table, my dad was just close enough to pick him up and throw him straight through the front window of Dale's bar.

A pair of cops happened to be outside in a police cruiser, just a few steps from the bar, right then. They were watching as the man came flying through the window. When they jumped out of their car, they saw Dad standing inside the bar window. They arrested him on the spot. However, quick-thinking Lara and Dale sent Mr. Pines out to represent Dad – right as he was being arrested!

Mr. Pines did some fast talking and even faster thinking. The bar didn't press charges, the man didn't press charges, and no one saw anything. The cops were sure they'd somehow been outmaneuvered, but there was nothing they could do about it, so they released Dad pending further investigation.

When my dad tried to pay Dale for the window. he refused to accept a penny, saying,

"That man fully deserved the licking you gave him." Dale laughingly said, "I figure the cost of that window was my price of admission to the show! I sure am glad Pines was here."

Mr. Pines said he wouldn't take Dad's money either. He told Dad that he felt obliged to represent Dad for his service to the morals of the community that night. Well, it's no great surprise that Dad and Mr. Pines became lifelong friends.

Often over the years, I would hear some reference to Dad and the bar like, "Mack, just how many times have you paid for that front window?" The comments were always in jest. While we were still kids, Dad would shush whoever was making the comment if either Deb or I were around. Years later, after I was an adult, Mom and Dad told me the whole story and I finally understood the genesis of the broken window joke.

Like I told you, there was nothing normal about our life, but it was our normal. Mom and Dad had decided to leave the hate, racism, and antisemitism of the south far behind and not look back. Dad was the most adamant about not raising racists, or allowing prejudice of any kind to influence us.

One of the biggest arguments I ever saw between my parents was when someone at the Ford factory did something my mother didn't like. In telling my father about the event, she resorted to her old south and used a racist word to make her point to Dad, with both of us girls within earshot.

My father was livid. He turned to us with his eyes blazing as he announced, "Girls, upstairs! Now!" All the excuses Mom tried to give him rang as hollow as an old dead tree. Dad, who never raised his voice to my mother, was furious. His cracking voice could be heard all over the house, "Ruby, you're speaking that hate you grew up with. You know damn good and well, I've seen the reality of what that talk can do. I won't have it! That'll not be around my girls! I mean it! I'll take them and leave! I can raise them just fine on my own!"

My parents were far from perfect, but they were trying to raise and I quote them, "a generation better." It was hours before my mother could restore the peace with my father. It finally came about the tenth time she said, "Mack, I'm so sorry! You're right. I'll do better by our girls, I promise." Peace was once again restored.

CHAPTER THIRTEEN

Not everything in my life would remain peaceful, though. In the following weeks, I realized that Nancy was becoming more and more aloof, unpredictable, and really, almost dangerous to be around. We'd be hanging out and she'd just start doing crazy things like swimming way out in the lake with all her clothes on, or tip over people's full garbage cans. Sometimes, she'd start to make crazy threats against girls she had decided she didn't like. She'd say things like, "Come on – we'll find her and shave her head!"

She had become totally unpredictable, was usually heavily drugged, and often acted spiteful. She'd even get nasty to me when I tried to talk to her about what she was doing. She would start yelling things like, "You're not my keeper!" When it began, I had no idea how bad things would become.

She had started running around with a couple of girls from town. Then I noticed that they were showing up at the Beach a lot. At some point, she stopped regularly slipping in our house at night to sleep. She would only appear once or twice for the remainder of the summer. Her erratic behavior left me with a great sense of loss and a lot of worry.

So, against my sister's wishes, I snuck out with a flashlight late one night, about four o'clock, and rode my ten-speed bike over to the area of the drug house. I had heard those strangers I had seen at the house before were from Toledo. I'm sure it was rented for the sole purpose of packaging and selling drugs. Dad always was screening his renters to avoid drug dealers. As for other landlords – well, I think they cared less about who they rented to.

I left my bike a few houses away and proceeded to sneak as quietly as I could up to the drug house from the back yards of other cottages. The house was dead quiet. I could see a really low light through the cracks of blanket-covered windows.

Being as stealthy as I could and keeping the flashlight pointed on the ground, I snuck up to the windows so I could peek in. No luck – the blankets were covering them completely. I was scared and silent as a mouse, but I kept slipping from one window to another. I was on a mission to see what was going on inside that place at night. Finally, I found one window where the blanket had slipped or been pulled back enough for me to see inside.

The first things that caught my eyes were a black light lava lamp and two candles, still lit but almost completely burnt out. Pools of wax covered the floor around them. Once I focused in on the room, there were needles, bent spoons, rubber tubes, pills, beer cans, and mostly empty liquor bottles. A little powder on the table was glowing in its foil. Everyone I could see seemed to be passed out.

Nancy and her girlfriends were on the floor, flopped up against two old broken dirty chairs. Johnny and Billy were against a wall. Johnny had a rubber tube around his forearm and a needle was still in his vein. Everyone was out cold. The older people, the ones I didn't know at all, were in the same condition. Some still had needles sticking in them and others had a rubber tube next to them, just flat on the floor. There must have been eight or nine people just in the living room. It looked like a bad zombie movie.

The air all around the house suddenly smelled different – dirty, and I was terrified by the filth I was seeing. The tears started to roll down my face as I raced away into the night. I had answered my question about what Nancy was up to – smack, heroin, horse, junk, call it what you want – hard fucking drugs ….

What I had seen that night told me two things, Nancy would never be the same and I would never be Nancy. For the next few days, I didn't see her, nor did I try. I was avoiding Johnny, Billy and everyone else. Everything in my world had been tainted with a stench, a horrible odor, the thought of which I couldn't get out of my mind.

I found some solace meeting Freddie on the beach in the early morning hours over the next weeks. He had even missed almost a week, out of his humiliation after the Barbara incident. However, I kept showing up at seven o'clock every morning, as planned, until he returned.

The seventh day after that horrible day that I saw Barbara's smelly socks and way too much more than I could wrap my head around, I saw him walking up the sand toward me. I just waved hard as he approached. He smiled and seemed relieved. We never spoke about Barbara and the towel. It was a bit of the elephant in the room with us, but we still hung out. When he was with me, we talked about the dreams we had, travel, and whatever else came into our minds.

He would hop on my motorcycle behind me, although he'd try his best to convince me to let him drive just about every time we rode somewhere. We would talk, and even though I told him what I had seen at the drug house, he still felt he needed to be friends with the boys. His attitude was, "Drugs won't get me!"

Getting nowhere with warning Freddie off hanging out with the boys, I changed the subject and asked him to a party in my garage. I told him about the plans that we had, with music and more. Freddie agreed to help me set up on Friday for that Saturday. Suddenly, I was looking forward to the set up more than the party.

On Friday, Freddie came over to help with the preparations at noontime. We listened to music as we got things ready. First, we covered some of the tools and the like with blankets to discourage Johnny and his gang from stealing stuff during the festivities. We set up tables, plasticware, and strung some Christmas lights for atmosphere. We worked for about two hours. Then, alone in the garage, he held my hand, brought me close to him and kissed me… it was almost like slow motion and so gentle.

Just then, our lips barely parted, we heard the cackle of the boys who had been peeking in the window, "Kiss, kiss!" Then all of the boys came storming into the garage laughing, "Tight Legs got kissed." Our private moment had been shattered. Sweet Freddie was first embarrassed, but then became all macho and yelled out, "Let's get out of here." They all took off together, leaving me behind.

On Saturday, everyone came to my party. There were maybe forty kids in the garage and driveway. Johnny and Billy teased Freddie and me a bit, but as soon as he put his macho face on, they let it die down for the day. Nancy was really stoned and drinking out of a bottle she hid in her purse. Johnny mostly stayed across the road from the far end of our driveway, smoking pot with Billy and Freddie. We all hung out, listening to music, dancing, and eating food. Then Nancy, Johnny, Billy, and Freddie all left suddenly.

Except for Freddie, they didn't seem to know I had seen what went on at the drug house, or they surely would have warned me not to tell anybody about what I saw. Freddie was honorable that way – I was sure he hadn't said anything to them. After all, I still had a crush on him. It seemed like initiation to the bad boys' club was losing your virginity! Freddie, thanks to Barbara, had become a full-fledged member of their little gang.

I found it nearly impossible to get the awful image of Barbara's filthy white socks with stripes around the ankle out of my mind. As for Freddie, our times of being together just slowly faded away.

One morning, on a rare occasion that Nancy had returned to stay a night, Dad was huddled in the kitchen talking to Deb and Hank. Nancy and I had woken up late and were watching TV. Hank came into the room and asked if we'd like to go shopping in town. We both jumped at the idea and rushed to get dressed.

Hank went into mom's bedroom to talk with her. Mom told her to get car keys and cash from her purse. Deb said she didn't want to go to town. Well, in a flash, Nancy and I were in the car ready to take off with Hank. Dad and Deb were getting into another car at the same time. I asked them where they were going. Dad said, "I just need to check about a little something."

Nancy and I usually would end our trips to town with Hank at the local hot dog drive-in, after shopping at Klines and other stores. That day was not an exception. As usual, Hank parked the car and we ate in it, after being served by a carhop. We were all having a great time, until someone who was parked next to us started their car to leave. On their way out, they called back to Hank, "What you doing with those White girls?"

Hank just ignored those folks. Nancy rolled down her window and called out from the back seat of the car, "Rednecks!" I silently agreed with her.

Even then, I knew the world was cruel. After all, I'd been called a honkey by Black girls before, so I knew it went both ways. Some days, simple human kindness is just absent, missing – it just gets lost in people's ignorance and stupidity.

Shortly after we returned home, we found out that another body had been found at the shoreline of one of the Beaches. If there had to be another body discovered, at least it wasn't in the community where we lived. It was near the area of the point, only a very few miles from Woodfield Beach.

This time, the body was a male in his twenties. My dad thought it was a guy he suspected of dealing drugs. Deb had told Dad that if it was Greg Van Marshall, she could confirm his ID for the police. Dad was reluctant, and tried to dissuade her. He kept asking, "You sure you want to do this?" Deb didn't hesitate, "Yes, I'm fine. If it's him, I'll know." Dad was concerned, "You've never seen a dead body close up." Deb shrugged. "I know, but it has to happen sooner or later."

My father wasn't happy at all about the prospect of Deb identifying the body. When they arrived at the morgue, Dad spoke alone with the officer who met them. After about a half hour, the officer returned with a driver's license picture. He announced that they had been able to confirm it was Greg Van Marshall without Deb having to see the body.

When Dad and Deb left the morgue, she told the cop, "He's a drug dealer from town. I've seen him around the Beaches. He's asked me if I was interested in buying speed or acid.

That's all I know." The officer spoke to Deb, "You didn't buy any drugs from him, right?" Without hesitation Deb replied, "Of course not! I don't ever use drugs. I'm not stupid." Dad laughed.

As they left in the car she told him, "Dad, I know more than I said to that cop." He pulled the car over. "Tell me everything you know." Deb said to him, "There's a house about ten streets over – I'm pretty sure the address is 2151 Lampdale Drive. I know some of the Beach kids are involved in what's going on. They're selling big quantities of pot, pills, and doing everything from hard liquor to heroin with a group of people about thirty."

Dad looked at Deb, "Does your sister know about it?" She didn't rat me out for going in the house, but she did tell him I said I peeked in the windows one night and told her what I saw. Dad looked at Deb, "How long have you known?" Deb shrugged, "Just a few days, really." Dad spoke firmly, "Enough said. Don't talk about any of this to anybody and I'll take care of it." Then they headed back onto the road toward home.

Dad made a call to another detective, one who had been assigned to the Greg case. They exchanged pleasantries for a minute, then Dad told him, "I've got some information, but it's gotta be anonymous, a 'no questions asked' kind of tip, Dave."

Detective Dave, who had known Dad for at least forever and a day, agreed. Dad told him everything he knew about what was going on at the drug house and gave him the exact address. Dad said he had double-checked the address because he needed to make sure the number was right. Detective Dave asked, "Is this all confirmed?" Dad replied, "Yes. The information's absolutely solid." The detective told Dad, "I'll go by and check it out now. We'll handle it. Thanks. I'll make sure to call you when it's going down"

In the very late afternoon, Dad drove Deb and me over every street in the Beach, searching everywhere to find Nancy. We saw her walking on the side of a road. Dad called to her and she came to the car window, "Get in, I'm taking you for pizza." At first Nancy, didn't want to go. However, Dad's face turned hard as he told her, "This isn't optional, Nancy." Surprised by his words, the tone of his voice, and his expression, her resistance evaporated and she got in the back seat with me without another word.

Later, that evening, the police busted the drug house and everyone inside. When the bust was happening, Nancy was with Deb and me at the pizza parlor, where Dad had dropped us off an hour before. He told us we might have to stay there a bit longer than usual, because he had an errand to run that might take a little while.

When he left us, he went to watch the bust from a distance. As it turned out, Hank picked all of us up. We found Dad sitting on the front porch and drinking coffee when we returned. Nancy was anxious to leave as soon as our feet barely hit the porch. "I've gotta get going."

Dad looked at the four of us standing on the sidewalk in front of him, "Just so you know, the sheriffs had a big drug bust over on Lampdale Drive." Nancy looked shocked and said, "I need to go home." Dad asked her if she wanted a ride. "No thanks, I'll walk. Bye." Off she went, headed in the direction of her house and not toward Lampdale Drive. I suppose she figured Dad knew what he was talking about.

Over the years, I've asked myself why I didn't see needle marks on her arms that summer. Well, here's the why and the how. Nancy and I would go our separate ways, but throughout the remainder of our lives, we would, from time to time, be in touch.

Our first reconnection would be about when we were twenty. It was, to say the least, not under the best of circumstances. While living in California, I heard that she was imprisoned in the California Institution for Women. I knew she had no family on the West Coast, so I made contact with the prison. Eventually, using a lot of patience, I found someone with the power to allow me to come see her.

I remember I wore pale yellow slacks and a blue and yellow shirt with cats on it. Why do I remember this? Well, it's the only time I've ever been inside, or even near a jail – or in this case a fucking prison. I wanted to look nice to give her hope.

I left my place in the early morning and walked all the way to the bus terminal to catch a Greyhound to the prison. I walked for about a mile. Then there was a lonely, two-hour-long ride from my home in Redondo Beach to the Chino area. California is a big state.

After a very long ride, the bus turned off the highway onto a dirt road. When the bus finally came to a stop, the driver said, "You're here – not many come this way mid-week. The weekends are busier." I was the only one getting off at that stop. As I exited, I replied, "I'm visiting an old friend." I looked at my watch; it was almost eleven o'clock. "The next bus going back is five this afternoon, right?" The driver smiled and said, "Yes, but don't miss it. It's the only one until tomorrow morning. Go that way to get to the prison," as he pointed across the road.

The area was nothing but a bus stop on one side of the dirt road. Another unpaved road intersected it on the other side. That's the direction the bus driver pointed. That road became a paved road as it approached a huge prison in the distance. It was hard to see much from the bus stop.

When I got off the bus, I was alone, all alone in the middle of nowhere. There was absolutely no one else anywhere around. I'll be honest, I was scared shitless.

The bus headed back toward the highway. After it left in a cloud of dust, I sat down at the small shelter and looked at the prison across the way. From a distance, it looked recently built. I noticed that the few trees along the dirt road weren't very tall. Within moments, the dust from the bus wheels had settled.

My next thought was that the air smelled remarkably fresh. My third thought was, "I wish I had worn flat shoes." I had started the day with a one-mile walk. In the city, I had walked the sidewalks barefoot most of the way, while carrying my cork-soled shoes with their four-inch box heels. That was not an option out here in the arid wilds.

Prison officials kept telling me I wasn't a relative, so I couldn't see her. I had persevered and finally won a months-long fight to get them to agree to let me see her. For the first time, sitting there at the bus stop, doubts were popping into my head. Did she even want to see me? Did they tell her I was coming? Which Nancy would greet me, the loving girl of my childhood or the erratic teen of her last drug-filled year with me? After all, it had been five years since I had seen her.

I stood up with all the courage I had in me and crossed the road and headed down the long dirt and paved road leading to the prison. I had no idea what I was walking into. I only knew what her crime had been. It was some sort of financial fraud crime.

CHAPTER FOURTEEN

When she was only seventeen, Nancy had followed some thirty-five-year-old guy to California. After they got there, he got her into this mess. She wasn't arrested for it until she was nineteen and back home in Michigan, in the Beaches. That must have been a hell of a surprise for her. She was extradited back to California, by airplane, in cuffs. It must have been a doozy of a five-finger discount jewelry shopping spree the two of them went on that Memorial Weekend....

An underage Nancy had committed the crimes with an older guy who doubtlessly convinced her to do it. Despite that, she was taken to court alone and accepted a plea bargain. Whoever Nancy's asshole criminal mastermind companion was, he was never charged, as far as I know.

I'll pull no punches. Nancy did commit the crimes; she told me herself. Even though she was a kid at the time, by the time they found, arrested, and charged her, she was of age. It still seems strange to me that Nancy was charged as an adult, since she was a juvenile when it all went down.

My best guess, knowing Nancy, is they threw the book at her because she would not flip on her criminal partner. And they sure did throw the book at her. She was a first offender and a juvenile when the crimes occurred, but she was sentenced to about three years in prison, as best I recall. She did about 18 months, because she got some time knocked off for good behavior.

As I walked up this horrifying road toward the prison, this was all the information that had been given to me. Would I see her through glass or bars? How long could I stay? When would I be able to leave? I had no idea what I was walking into. Now, if you have ever read a book where someone goes to visit a prison or mental hospital and the authorities keep them … that was just a small part of the thoughts racing through my head.

As I approached the prison, there was one security station after another and guards at checkpoint after checkpoint, all along the road. I started going through checkpoints long before I even got close to the prison walls.

Before long, I realized that the towers I had seen from the bus stop were guard towers for armed snipers. Then I began to see fences fortified with barbed wire.

They were all reasonably nice to me at the multiple check points. Repeatedly, I was asked for the same information – "ID, purpose of visit, prison contact person," in very matter-of-fact, business-as-usual tones. If I hadn't been so darned nervous, I would have taken some comfort in the guards' demeanors. They obviously weren't very concerned at all about little old me. I guess they didn't think I had that John Dillinger jailbreaker look.

Finally, after making it past all of the security checks, I approached the building, expecting to enter the biggest iron double doors I had ever seen. They were very new and really quite amazing – almost artistic. I guess, at least for that moment, they weren't utterly terrifying to me. As so often happens, the truth turned out to be much more ordinary.

A guard directed me to a regular door beside the enormous iron doors. As I walked through that door, a woman dressed in a suit met me. She introduced herself and said she was Nancy's prison counselor. Then she told me I would need to be searched and guided me into a room. "Put your purse in this locker." I followed her instructions. "Go in there and pass all of your clothes out – everything."

I entered a small stall with a door. It was partitioned off like some public toilet stalls, with an open view low to the ground and above the door. I passed my clothing out. I assume she searched my clothes, because after a few seconds, she opened the door, looked at me standing naked, and then handed my clothes back to me. I redressed.

When I came out, she told me to open the locker. Then she emptied the contents of my purse on a table and examined everything, one at a time. The woman said, "You asked about showing her a picture of your baby. That's fine. Oh – and I see you have cigarettes and matches, Nancy is allowed to smoke – so if you would like to bring them with us, you can. Hand all of the items you want to take with you to me."

I took a picture of my daughter and picked up a sealed pack of cigarettes and a book of matches, then passed them to the counselor. She looked at the matches, opened them, and then opened the cigarettes.

Next, she took me into a small office. She explained, "You have been granted access for this visit for one reason and one reason only. When I informed Nancy about your repeated requests to see her, I told her, "One of your partners in crime, Claudette, is trying to visit you." Her reply made all the difference to me, "Claudette! That's the straight side of me!" I smiled and laughed, "It's true."

She went on to tell me, "We are in one of the rehabilitation areas of the prison. Nancy's in minimum security and she has done very well. We don't want anyone interrupting her progress. She has had no visitors and very few letters since she arrived thirteen months ago. I trust you won't say or do anything to cause her a setback. If it looks that way to me, I'll terminate your visitation. You'll be allowed to hug her once when you first see her and one more time as you leave. Other than that, it's hands off. This way, please."

The first thing I noticed as we headed through the prison was how quiet, clean and very modern it was. It was almost like walking on the floor of a very quiet office building, except that all the people who passed by and nodded were wearing prison guards' uniforms marked "CIW."

185

The prison complex was huge. We would pass through doors that led outside, and then through more doors that took us back into the buildings. Everything seemed so peaceful. In fact, very few people were even visible at all.

Finally, we arrived at a gymnasium-sized room with maybe forty tables – each with four chairs attached to it – and no one else in the room. It was immaculately clean and as quiet as an empty church. The counselor stood to the front near the door we had entered. She passed me the photo, cigarettes, and matches, and told me to take a seat at the only table with an ashtray. It was about twenty feet from the entrance. Then she picked up a wall phone.

Within a few minutes, I saw Nancy in the distance, as she entered from a door on the far side of the room. She came in alone, dressed in grey sweats, happily approaching the aisle, on her way to me. She was just like I'd known her in our early childhood days. She grinned widely as she called out, "Claudette!"

Nancy called the counselor by name, and asked only one word, "Hug?" The counselor nodded and we hugged tight for a long time and then sat down. Nancy's first words to me were, "How did you find me?" I told her Dad had gotten word about her to me. Of course, she immediately started asking questions about everybody, even as we were sitting down across from each other. When Nancy saw the cigarette pack on the table, she pointed toward it as she looked questioningly at the counselor. The woman nodded her approval, so each of us lit a cigarette.

Within an instant, Nancy picked up the picture of my daughter from the table and looked at it for a long time, "She's beautiful! I love her already." She held onto the photo as we talked. After a while, she asked if she could keep the photo. My response was, "Of course, but get permission first – we don't want to do anything that will keep you from getting out of here as soon as you can."

Nancy motioned for the counselor and she approached the table. Nancy showed her the photo, "Can I keep this?" The counselor smiled and nodded, saying, "Your friend can't hand the picture directly to you to keep, but I can hold it and then give it to you after she leaves." Nancy handed her my daughter's photo, "Thank you."

As our afternoon went on, Nancy told me what led her to a life as a prisoner. She even commented that she was fat because, "I'm off heroin!" I then asked about the things that had been preying on my mind since I learned of her addiction. "How did I miss the needle marks on you that last summer we were together? Maybe I could have . . ." She stopped me right there, "No. Don't even go there!" I was still shooting up in my feet at that time. There's no way you could have seen. I did this to me, not you, and no one could have stopped me back then."

She asked about my life, so I told her about it as the hours passed. She told me of her plans for when she got out – and the main one was, "Never go to jail again!" She assured me she was fine. After all, she had only months left on her sentence and, of course, she was a model prisoner. I don't know if I entirely believed she was fine – after all, she was in prison – but I wanted to believe it, and for everything she was telling me to be true.

Only the day before, the prison people told her that authorization had been granted for me to see her and that I was coming to visit the very next day. That said, being Nancy, she had already gotten special permission to take me to see her "private room" … that's what she called her cell. The counselor and a CIW guard walked with us down hallways and through doors leading throughout the prison. As we approached higher security areas, the noise got louder and louder, and then it waned as we passed.

In one area, women were calling out and heckling me like I was a freak on display. One yelled, "Ooh, baby! You here for me and here to stay?" Nancy quickly said, "Just ignore them." Then we passed through one more thick metal door, and it was quiet again. Within seconds, we arrived at an open solid door with a tiny window inside it, leading to a six by eight-foot cell.

The counselor and guard stood across the narrow hall from the wide-open door. The guard looked at me and said, "You can go in." Nancy proudly showed me her tiny cell.

It was modern, freshly painted white, sparkling clean, and tidy. Nancy had books and magazines carefully arranged on a shelf. Images cut from magazine pages had become her artwork, taped neatly to the wall. She had a little vanity area that hid the toilet. There were a few items of makeup on top of it. Everything was folded and absolutely neat, "See, Claudette? I'm perfectly fine – I even have a private room. Besides, I'll be out of this place in a few months! I can't stay here when I get out – I'll have to go back home to serve my parole time."

As we walked back, she told me, "I know what a big trip this was for you. Don't try to do it again. You don't belong here. I'll be out soon." I asked her if there was anything I could do for her, "If you can leave enough for a pack of cigarettes or two for me at the prison commissary, that would be great."

I told her I had fifty dollars I'd leave for her, "No, no – that's too much! You can't afford that – after all, you have a baby to take care of!" She was right, I couldn't. However, I just looked at her and said, "There will be a fifty in your commissary account when I leave." We hugged goodbye. I could tell that Nancy didn't want my visit to end, but she knew the rules – our time was limited. With tears in her eyes, her last words to me that day were, "You're the only visitor I've had. I love you." I told her, "I love you, too."

In due course, Nancy was released from prison and became the world's best parolee. Throughout our lives, our paths would cross. Or maybe a random phone call would come, straight out of the blue, from one of us to the other. We always seemed to find each other.

By then, my daughter was growing up – so the rules had to be firm. No drugs or alcohol were allowed in my house when Nancy came to visit. I generally didn't keep alcohol in the house anyway, but if there was any, it was disposed of before she arrived.

It's not that I never had alcohol in my home – but never, ever was there even a drop of it around when Nancy was coming to visit. She knew not to bring anything – drugs or alcohol – with her. She loved my daughter and willingly obeyed my strict house rules.

Looking back on it, there were some good and bad years for Nancy, but overall, her life was steadily moving in a direction that I never wanted for her. Alcohol would haunt her life and ruin her health.

In the better years, she would come to visit on a Sunday from time to time and clean my house, just for the hell of it. She knew I worked a lot, and she wanted to help – and she did. It wasn't that she wanted anything to do with family life, it was because she just wanted to help me out.

191

Once she told me this unforgettable line on why she didn't want children, "I'd rather put diamonds on my fingers than shoes on a baby." You may find her statement cold. I didn't. It was honest – it was Nancy's type of brutal candor. Nancy also threatened me once, even though she said it with a laugh. She said that if she ever got pregnant, she was going to leave the baby at my door. I didn't appreciate that statement at all, because I knew she was not kidding!

That's partly because of how I think about raising children. It's my opinion that once you have a child, you will, and should aways be, taking second place in your own life. Your child must come first. I didn't have Jimmy Choo heels, but my daughter always wore Buster Browns.

Once in a great while, as adult single women, Nancy and I would go dancing or out to dinner. We went from rock to disco to whatever came next. Maybe once every year or three, or after a few more years apart, we would find ourselves living in the same town.

I even talked her into going to real estate school with me. Perhaps surprisingly, she was on time every morning at eight o'clock sharp.

However, she was also toting a slushy cup filled with vodka and cranberry juice. We both passed the course and got our licenses! But she only worked in real estate for a month or two before she quit. To be fair, I didn't care for the work very much, either.

The last night we went out together, it was to dinner and then a dance club in Clearwater, Florida. Nancy drove us to a nightclub called Studebaker's. I had chosen the club because I had found it quite pleasant on the couple of occasions I had been there before.

As its name implied, Studebaker's had an automotive theme, with booths made of car trunks that had been turned into benches. It had good food, and in the evenings, neon lightings were prominently displayed. It was a club that appealed to local business people, so I thought it was a good choice as a place for us to go for dinner and drinks.

During the evening, I went to the ladies' room, only to find Nancy selling cocaine in there. She turned, looked at me and said, "I'm not doing it, just selling!" Pissed, I said, "You had that in your car with me inside! I'll take a cab home." She followed me out and said, "I'm sorry." I took that cab.

She did kick heroin, as far as I know. But still, she had a lifelong battle with alcohol, pills, and even cocaine. She remained my friend, from a distance, as time went on in our two very different lives.

She flew in to see me on my fiftieth birthday, as a surprise. It was wonderful, but more than a little sad. Throughout our adult life, I had been able to control her, to keep her from drinking to excess or taking drugs when she was around me. However, it had been ten years or more since I had seen her. We simply talked on the phone a few times a year just to stay in touch.

I knew things were not good for her, but only when she visited me did I understand how bad things had actually become. She drank nonstop for the week she was with me – even I couldn't slow her down. If I refused to take her to the store for alcohol, she said, "I'll walk." She was never falling-down drunk, just consistently drunk, drinking from her first sip of booze when she woke up until her last sip as she went to sleep.

Sometime around our fifty-seventh year of life, she phoned me. It was a Wednesday that she called, I think. We talked for hours about her declining health from years of substance abuse and about our bubblegum sun days. She always seemed to know which of the Beach kids made it with a nice family life, or great career, or both – and who ended up on drugs, in prison, or dead.

I could tell she was drinking heavily that night, and I even asked her about it. She said, "Fuck it, you know I'm gonna drink. But no drugs – really! I'm happy." The call we were dreading came just a few days later. While having another medical procedure, her heart gave out. Nancy was gone.

Now I have told you about two of the Beach kids. We were a pair who were friends for fifty-one years. Even though our lives led us in different directions, our fast friendship endured. So, let's go back to teenage life under the bubblegum sun …

CHAPTER FIFTEEN

One Friday afternoon over at the shack, Billy, Deb, Sharon, Gate, and I were hanging around. Johnny showed up with news about the corpse on the beach. "The papers confirm the body was Greg Van Marshall. They say it was an overdose, but they're investigating."

Billy looked at Johnny, "Well, I guess you don't have to worry about the money you owed him!" Johnny looked hard at Billy, "I paid that back; besides I was here with you all that day when he was killed, or whatever day. Right?" Without hesitation, Billy concurred. "Yeah, yeah, buddy, we were together."

This happened around the time that Dad's concerns about the drugs and deaths at the lakes made him to worry about "his girls." When it came to our safety, Dad was on top of everything going on in the area. Over the preceding two weeks, Deb had overheard a few whispers about Dad wanting to sell all his property and move us to town. Mom and Dad were not talking to us about this move, but we

196

noticed they were slipping away without us. We were sure they were looking for houses somewhere in town.

Hank must have been sworn to silence. She wouldn't say a word to us about it, no matter how much we questioned her, the response we got was, "Really, I haven't heard anything about it." We were pissed. It seemed they only talked when we were upstairs. Deb was furious; she wasn't leaving Ronnie!

We were desperate for information. So, one Saturday morning, with Deb downstairs and me upstairs, I called the operator to call us back for a line check. When the phone rang back, I answered upstairs and Deb answered downstairs. I thanked the operator and she disconnected, leaving the line open. Deb kept the line open downstairs and put the phone receiver under the couch, right at the edge. I kept the upstairs line open. That way, we could use the telephones like an intercom to spy on our parents!

We had first learned about this by accident. Over the years we had called into radio station game shows like CKLW's. Since there were several extension phones in the house, both of us could be in on the call. If one of us didn't know the answer to a question, the other one might. Or we'd make prank calls to stores, asking things like, "Do you have Prince Albert in the can?" Some poor sucker of a shopkeeper would answer, "Yes." Then we'd cackle, "Better let him out!" Those calls were too good not to share!

However, it was when we'd call for the operator to tell us what time it was that we realized that the phones would work as a microphone system. Of course, we had never used it on our parents before that day, but we knew it worked just from playing around over the years. This, my friends, is old school tech!

Deb raced upstairs. We waited, listening carefully as our parents entered the living room. We kept a cloth over the microphone part of the handset, so our unsuspecting parents wouldn't hear a stray noise and get wise to what we were doing. We could tell that our parents had been in ongoing discussions. Mom was first, "How long do you think it'll take to sell? After all, school's coming up."

Dad told her, "Mr. Bornstein has always been interested. Pines says if we package the properties we'll lose money, but it can all be done quickly. So, what about that house on

Arbor Avenue – okay?" Mom was firm, "Yes. Do it!" Dad looked out the window. "Okay, I'll get it done. Looks like Pines is here – I'll take him across the street to talk."

Deb and I heard every word. They were selling our house and moving us! Even though when they approached us a while back, we told them, "Absolutely not, we don't want to leave the Beach!" To make things worse, they weren't even discussing it with us. We girls had made it more than clear to them – there was no way we would willingly move to town! Obviously, no one was listening to what we had to say except us.

Deb raced downstairs and I followed, out the door and across the street to the green house. Dad and Mr. Pines were already inside the house, talking with the windows wide open. We could hear Dad say, "Package them up – check with Bornstein, he may want to buy all of them in a package deal."

Mr. Pines told Dad, "Like I said, you'll lose money, but I don't blame you. So, you like the house in town?" Dad said, "Yeah, Ruby says it's fine. Hank is happy to go with us." Mr. Pines hesitated a little, then he said, "You know, all those White folks in that

199

neighborhood certainly will not take kindly to anyone having a Black woman around."

Dad shook his head, saying, "Ruby talked to Hank and she said, 'Hell, we tamed all the racists here, so we'll just handle the ones in town, too.' You know how Hank is." Mr. Pines paced across the living room floor, "I still don't think that's a good idea for Hank."

Squatting outside the window, Deb was getting madder and madder, and then she suddenly blew up! She stood up, no longer hiding by the window where we had been doing our eavesdropping. She started pacing, moving back and forth in front of the open window, while waving her arms in the air.

Dad and Mr. Pines could clearly see her rage, "You tell him, Mr. Pines! That part of town – Arbor Avenue? Yes Dad, we know all about your plan! It's not safe for Hank! Town is divided as it gets, Whites on the West Side and Blacks on the East Side! No Hank . . . I can tell you, Mom's not moving without her! I'm sure in the hell not leaving and Claudette isn't going either. So, you better talk to Mom again before you sign any damn papers!" She marched back and forth in front of the window in an emotional tailspin!

Dad and Mr. Pines just let her blow off steam. Finally, Dad just said, "Enough! Go home. Both of you." Mr. Pines looked at Dad, "Mack, I think you have a problem with your older one, but she's right about Hank and the dividing line. Just think about it and let me know what you want me to do." Dad looked unwaveringly at Mr. Pines as he firmly uttered, "Do it."

Deb already was mad and had started to plan a counter attack, but when she heard what Dad and Mr. Pines were saying, she was fully on the warpath. Trust me, that's not something you'd ever want to see! Easygoing Deb had quite a temper. We headed straight up to our room with her rage in full swing. She was shrieking, "We've got to confirm the plans, reset the balance!"

Deb reached under her bed and pulled out a thick envelope. She waved it in the air and then she winked at me, saying, "Tomorrow, we'll activate our plan. We'll tell Dad to take us for lunch pizza to talk. You know what to do. Just follow my lead. We're ready!"

The next day, we sat across from Dad and, despite ourselves, let him slowly talk us into the move. Ultimately, we quietly surrendered.

Deb looked at me and then back to Dad, "It'll be fine, Dad – we'll adjust. How about you drop us off in town so we can get a better lay of the land? Just for a few hours."

Dad's face showed pure relief, and he quickly agreed. He dropped us off in town and said he would pick us up at six. We had four hours! As soon as Dad's car was out of sight, we walked down the main street of the town, then cut into an alley. We stopped and I looked at my watch, "Go!"

Deb quickly spun her hair into a twist with a comb, just like she had practiced in our room. She put on red lipstick and then pulled a suit jacket and big Jackie O sunglasses out of her purse. In minutes, she looked hot, sexy, and twenty-one! She looked at me, "Did you time me?" I began laughing, "A new record – under two minutes!" We headed straight for the bus station.

Deb entered the bus station, walking in like she owned the place. A few heads turned at the gorgeous woman. I followed about thirty seconds behind her, and took a seat near twenty-some people who were waiting for a bus. Deb was already next in line. She walked up to the window with a slip of paper.

Reading from it, she said, "I'd like a one-way ticket to San Francisco, Saturday the twenty-sixth. Departure time is about 6 a.m., I believe." The man smiled big at Deb and then looked at the schedule, "Yes, 6:10. That'll be $37.50, please."

Deb handed him forty dollars from her purse. He gave her change and the ticket. Smiling, she put the money and ticket in her purse as she said, "Thank you." The ticket agent was clearly checking her out as he said, "You're welcome. Have a good trip!" He continued to stare at her as she walked away. Deb walked right past my seat. I got up and followed her outside a few seconds later.

About a block away, we sat on the grass in a park and she pulled the ticket out, "We got it!" I said through a grin, "You were fantastic!" We both laid back on the grass laughing. Deb took a Kleenex out of her purse and wiped the lipstick off. Then she removed her jacket, her shades, and let her hair down. The last thing she did was move her Angela Davis pin from her waistband, where it had been covered by her jacket, back to her blouse.

After we both looked at the ticket for a while, Deb put it inside the brown envelope in

203

her purse. I smiled broadly saying, "You did it!" She laughed, "We did it! Come on, let's get some rice pudding at the diner."

We sat for hours in a back booth, talking quietly. In 1967, all you needed to buy a bus ticket was to look eighteen. No ID was needed and no one ever asked for it, least of all, the bus station employee that day. Of course, Deb always looked older with her hair up, and to be honest, the guy behind the counter was too busy looking at the pretty woman ….

Well, that's exactly what we had counted on. Deb and I had practiced that change of clothes in our room. We both practiced it, even though I was still too young to pull off looking like an adult. After all, we weren't sure how much time we would have, if and when the day came that we would need to use that trick. As it happened, there was no need to rush, but I timed her anyway.

With a silk blouse and jeans on, she just needed the jacket and attitude. However, she refused to take off her Angela Davis pin. She pinned it to the waist of her jeans, where the jacket would hide it. Like I told you before, she was never fully dressed until she was wearing that pin somewhere!

CHAPTER SIXTEEN

Two days later, at 1:30 in the morning, the police came knocking at our front door. Dad looked out the window and saw the unmarked police vehicle. He saw Detective Martin and Detective James standing on the porch. Dad knew both of them well, and opened the front door to see what they wanted.

"Guys?" Then he barely stepped through the doorway onto the porch. Mom, who had gotten up right after Dad, got to the door in time to hear the words, "Mack, we have some really bad news. Henrietta is dead." Mom, dressed in her elegant nightgown, gasped as she opened the door. Dad caught her as she stumbled onto the porch exclaiming, "Dear Lord, she left a few hours ago! My God! Have Claire and the family been told?" Detective Martin nodded, "Yes, we were just there."

Mom looked like she was going to pass out. Dad grabbed Mom and held her up as he asked, "What the hell happened? Sit down." Dad guided Mom to a chair and they all sat on the porch. Detective Martin told Dad, "It was a train track accident. Her car was hit at the Albain Road crossing." Mom, coming to her senses, asked, "You're sure it was Hank? Why would she be there this late?" Dad looked at Mom as the cops answered with their silence. Mom got up and headed into the house, "I need to call Claire."

Dad asked the policemen, "Anyone else in the car?" Detective James told him she was alone. Dad, who was still trying to get his head around it, said, "Was the car stalled? That's a new car – it shouldn't have stalled." Detective James told him, "We're investigating now. You knew her well – is there any chance it could have been suicide?" Dad looked hard at the two men, "No way!" Detective Martin nodded, "I didn't think that would be the answer to what happened." Dad said to the detectives, "She was one of the happiest folks I've ever known." Detective Martin told him, "We're checking the lights and warning signals, trying to figure it out."

Dad was really upset. "You gotta do more than just that – look at everything, including foul play, 'cause she wouldn't normally be in that area." Detective Martin knew exactly where Dad's head was, "We will, but we don't expect any developments along those lines. There hasn't been any racial tension in that area recently, but we'll look at everything – I promise you, Mack."

The men left. Mom and Dad sat down at the kitchen table. As Mom was putting a coffee cup in front of Dad, she said, "We need to wake the girls." Dad picked up his cup, "No, Ruby – we'll wait until morning." Then they both heard us stirring around upstairs. "Mack, I think they're awake." Dad nodded, "Let's just wait. If they come down, we'll tell them."

A few minutes later, Deb and I, still half asleep, came down the stairs. It didn't take us long, with the porch and kitchen light on, to realize that something was up. We groggily stumbled through the house and into the kitchen, "What's going on?" Dad said, "Sit down, we need to tell you something." We were both waking up fast – Dad was way too serious. Puzzled, we took a seat at the table. Then we noticed that Mom had tears welling up in her eyes.

Dad told us the horrible news as gently as he could. The news left both of us devastated and in tears. I cried out, "She just left in her pretty sequined blue dress!" The thought of her getting killed in that dress was devastating for me. The horrible news about her death made for a very rough night for all of us.

The investigation concluded that the trees around the track had obstructed her view and with music on and all of the windows closed tight, she just didn't hear the train. Hers was simply an accidental death.

The funeral was a graveside service that happened at the East Side Cemetery on Friday. It was attended by Hank's family, including a devastated Claire. Mr. Bornstein and Mr. Pines were there, and so was Nancy. Many of Hank's friends from the factory, maybe a hundred all told, both Black and White, were present for the service. Even the detectives, a few officers, and some of Dad's friends attended. Of course, our whole family was there, too. I tried not to cry, but I don't think I succeeded.

Afterwards, we stopped by a reception and meal at a church. We brought food, as is the custom, but mostly we went there to pay our respects to the family. Nancy seemed really uncomfortable. She ate nothing and decided to get an early ride back to the Beach.

Later that afternoon, when we got back to the Beach from the funeral, I took my motorcycle for a ride. I wanted to travel every road, hoping that the wind in my face would clear my head. It really didn't work.

It wasn't long before I stumbled on Nancy, Freddie, Johnny, Gate, Billy, and a few others. They were huddled around the rocks on the beach, smoking a glass pipe and drinking. Nancy was so high she fell in the sand just getting up. That day, another thing became crystal clear to me. Freddie had become part of the Beach's hard drug culture.

When I saw what was happening, I just rode on. There was already too much pain for one day – I surely didn't need more. I pulled into our garage late that evening. I filled the bike's gas tank and then went up to our room, where Deb was resting on the bed.

Deb and I spent the remainder of the evening in our room. Because of the funeral, Mom had gone to work late for her afternoon shift at Ford. Dad was getting ready to hit the midnight shift. He would leave about – well, exactly – at nine-forty at night and return home at six-twenty in the morning. Mom wouldn't be home until one o'clock, so we had some time alone. That suited us perfectly, especially that night.

At four in the morning, with Mom long since home and fast asleep, Deb and I grabbed a large backpack and a duffel bag. Quietly, even though we knew Mom slept like a rock, we left the house through the utility room door and tiptoed out into the back yard, being careful to close and lock the door without making the slightest sound.

The fog was thick as we approached the sidewalk heading toward the garage. The temperature outside was barely sixty degrees, unusually cool, even for late August. The temperature and the dampness in the air made us glad we both had worn coats. We headed down the sidewalk to the small garage door. Deb unlocked it and said, "I'll meet you on the other side." She walked around the garage, carrying the bags.

I took my motorcycle out of the small door as quietly as possible and turned the lock, before heading toward the back street, past the still closed big garage door. Deb was waiting with the back gate open. I told her to stack the bags on my bike and we'd roll it together. We rolled the loaded bike outside the gate and locked the gate again. Then, with one of us on each side, we started pushing the motorcycle down the road toward the lake without turning the motor on. We quickly realized the ground wasn't very wet at all. Most of what we thought was fog was actually smoke from the factories rolling our way.

Our biggest concern was the neighbors who might already be leaving for work. They would find our actions unusual and could possibly stop by the house to talk to Mom and Dad. That had been Deb's biggest worry for weeks. Not a car passed us as we approached the lake area, and we didn't see many lights on inside the houses.

We sat on the breakwall next to the clubhouse, between the grassy knoll and the water. The motorcycle was parked on the sand. The backpack and duffel bag rested between us. Deb was going over the details of the plan. I looked at her, "Just remember, rule one – you can always call Dad, he's always willing to forgive." She laughed.

Deb peered at her watch as she said, "They'll be here soon." I looked at the backpack and duffel bag on the ground. "Got everything?" Deb looked in the duffel bag, pulled out a brown envelope, looked inside it, and then put the envelope into the backpack. "All good." I winked at her. "You scared?" She smiled, saying, "No, I got this! Scared? No way! I'm excited!"

Ronnie's Chrysler pulled up to the horseshoe drive of the clubhouse, just behind where we were seated. We stood up as the car came to a stop. I hugged her and told Deb I loved her. She smiled, "Love you too, Kiddo. Be safe." Ronnie had opened the car door for Deb. Four others, three more guys and one girl, were already waiting in the car. Ronnie called out to Deb, "Come on, we gotta go!"

Deb grabbed her duffel bag, slung it over her shoulder, and headed toward the open car. She turned back to me, watching from the lake. Then she flashed me the peace sign. I called out, "March on!"

I watched as they pulled away. When I could no longer see the car, I sat back down on the breakwall. It took a moment to sink in – Deb was really gone. A wild pink coneflower was in full bloom right beside me. I took it as a sign. I smiled, stood up, undid my braids, and fluffed my hair out. Then I bent over and picked the flower, attaching it in my hair with a barrette I had in my pocket. I looked at my watch. It read ten minutes past five, still too early for there to be even a hint of daylight.

Without a moment's hesitation, I strapped on the backpack, jumped on my motorcycle and took off down the sand at the water's edge toward town. By then, the moon was shining brightly in the sky again. For some completely illogical reason, I didn't fear what laid ahead.

This was a trip I had only made a few times – all the way to town. My plan was to stick to the beachfront as long as possible. Then there were fields I could cross, followed by small roads and empty highways that took me all the way to town.

I parked my motorcycle in a spot where Dad would find it and kept the key, knowing he had an extra. I boarded the 6:10 bus to San Francisco. I didn't look back, knowing in my heart I was headed for what would certainly be the greatest adventure of my life. That really is exactly what I thought.

Dad arrived home, as normal, at six-twenty that morning. He was dead tired. Because Mom was still sleeping, he was being careful not to wake her and missed seeing our letter on the fireplace mantel. Later, I would find out it was almost nine-thirty before they knew what we had done. Although the letter didn't say where we were going, Dad had some idea where we were by the next day.

It was common knowledge that groups were leaving in cars to organize a large march in Washington, DC. Of course, later in the following day, the police called Dad about finding my motorcycle. Then he was really worried, and he had all sorts of questions swirling in his head. Were we in a car on the way to Washington, or going by bus? Was Washington our destination?

Dad ended up having to send someone into Washington to find us. His only lead was some crumpled-up papers that had the name Deborah Ann Nealy, age twenty-two. I guess they were some of my practice documents. I was a great forger – at least for her ID!

Sometimes, our misdeeds come back to bite us. I need to tell you how that fake ID would end up coming back to haunt two sisters traveling for business about thirty-two years later. In 1999, we were traveling cross-country together, passing through an area just south of Tupelo, Mississippi.

Deb was a slow, careful driver, and still a night owl. It made perfect sense for her to do the driving for the night shift. That night, I was asleep in the passenger seat of my Lincoln Town Car. It all started to happen at about four in the morning.

A police officer turned on his flashing lights to pull over our car. Deb gently touched my arm. "Kiddo wake up, I'm getting pulled over." Just coming out of my sleep, I was still groggy but waking up fast. "You? You're a turtle." She stopped on the side of the road and rolled her window down.

The officer got out and approached the car. He asked for her license and registration and stood at the window for a moment, "You were going 5 miles over the speed limit, but I also noticed you were weaving. Have you had anything to drink?" Shocked by his question, "No, of course not," Deb answered. Then he asked, "Whose car is this?"

Now, I really was waking up, "Deb does not drink and it's my car. Weaving? This road is full of potholes!" The officer told us, "Wait here." Deb and I were busy talking about how ridiculous this stop was and how, maybe when it was over, we'd grab an early breakfast.

However, the officer returned shortly and requested my driver's license to verify that I was the owner of the car. Irritated, I handed it to him, "Yes, the car's mine." The officer left again. Deb and I were waiting, truly puzzled.

The officer returned to the car window one more time, "Both of you out of the car. Step to the rear." We really had no idea what in the hell was going on at that point. After all, it was four in the morning, and there we were, two women all alone on a rural Mississippi highway. We were both getting extremely worried about what could possibly happen next. After all, everything about the stop was weird. I gave Deb a look and nodded. She knew that meant for her to watch this guy. We complied with his demand, while carefully observing every move the officer was making.

With both of us standing at the back of the car, he nosed around the inside of my car, "No weapons or drugs? I told him, "No. We're traveling on business from a diamond market trade show that finished in New York this afternoon. We're just businesswomen trying to get home, nothing else."

He paused for a minute, still looking at our licenses, then looked hard at both of us.

Then he held one license out, "The name on this driver's license shows an alias, Deborah Ann Nealy. NCIC is showing an old prior arrest in Washington, DC. There's still an outstanding arrest warrant for failure to appear for court under that name."

Deb and I looked at each other with our mouths wide open. It all came rushing back. We started laughing – I mean out loud, belly-laughs, with tears rolling down our faces. We simply couldn't stop laughing.

I'm sure that officer thought that we had completely lost our minds. At that moment, I don't think either of us gave a shit what the cop thought or about the potential for her being arrested right there and then. Really, any good lawyer could sort out the mess – and if we went to jail that night, at least we would be together. After all, we could take one more for the civil rights movement.

At first, the officer was taken aback by our reaction and his face showed a moment of confusion. Then he got so worked up that he was almost snarling. However, when he finally realized that we simply couldn't stop laughing and didn't give a damn, he began to figure out that there was something more going on. He said, "I'll wait – this must be a hell of a story!"

Eventually, we calmed down enough to tell him of the sisters' great escape of 1967, the march on Washington, the flower children of San Francisco, and more. By that point, he was laughing with us. "Love it! My God, that's the best story I've heard in years! I can't wait to tell my mama – she was part of the movement here in Mississippi! I'll tell you, it's those darned computers – they're catching everything nowadays. You are both lovely ladies, so go you just go on – I'll annotate the NCIC system. This shouldn't happen again."

Anyway, back to that summer of '67, so long ago, Deb would be the first person busted – twice! First, she was arrested by the police in DC for organizing an upcoming march and then snitched out by Dad's private eye, who located her at the jail. The PI found Deb incarcerated and charged as an adult, under the name Deborah Ann Nealy.

All the women prisoners of conscience in the overcrowded cells knew that Deb was underage, and so they were all giving her their cartons of milk and their cookies. She said they were a lovely group of ladies, and they took great care of her for the very few days that she lived the life of a woman in chains. The entire timespan for Deb's great escape was a whopping twelve days.

The PI called Dad to tell him about Deb. That was the moment Dad first knew I wasn't with Deb. It didn't take long for her to be convinced that I could be in great danger. Much later, she admitted that she had been worried about me the entire time she was in Washington. When Dad talked to her on the phone, Deb spilled the beans. She informed him that I was in San Francisco. To say that my folks blew their tops about my adventure was an enormous understatement. In our later conversations, Deb said that she'd never heard him anywhere near as angry as he had been during that telephone call.

Deb was able to calm Dad down a bit by telling him a little more of the truth. She knew that I had taken more than a thousand dollars from our savings with me for my trip to San Francisco. She told him about the money and that I could be found at the library every day at two in the afternoon. Dad was glad I had enough money to survive, but then he got worried that I might get swindled out of my money, or even robbed.

219

I don't know if Dad was more or less mad when she told him we had worked out a detailed plan together, called a rooming house to arrange housing, and about our many safety precautions. But, anyway, before very long at all, they found me, too. I was already hoping for some way to peacefully surrender. I missed Mom and Dad, and I really, really missed my sister. I was ready to go home, and they wanted me back. Dad told me so when he got there to pick me up. He already had tickets for us on the next available flight to Detroit. The total elapsed time during my escape was a whopping fourteen days.

However, I'll tell you, it was cool as shit! That part of California had rolling hills, the Golden Gate Bridge and the most beautiful architecture I have ever seen. I rode the trolly cars from one end of the city to the other, laughing and amazed. I even made friends with some of the flower children on the streets. No one there knew where I was staying or that I actually had money. That was also a part of Deb's plan. I knew that one day, I would come back to that wonderful city by the bay.

We both returned, not to the Beaches we loved so dearly, but to the house on Arbor Avenue. We arrived there before the furniture was even unpacked. We'd fought a fierce battle not to leave the Beaches that were always our home. However, we lost the war.

While he is driving me, Jay tells me that after I left the area for good, the folks on the Beach chased off all the drug dealers, and things started to get back to the way they had been before the druggies took over. He says the environmental cleanup has worked, too. The Beaches are clean again, and except for blooms of algae off and on in Lake Erie, the water looks clear, too. He tells me that it's almost back to the way it was when we were Beach kids. He says he's glad he stuck it out, but he certainly understands why I left.

As for the Beach kids I grew up with, I can tell you here that Johnny ended up in prison for life, charges unknown, maybe as a habitual offender or for murder, I have no idea which one. Billy and Gate seem to survived and managed to get off drugs. And dear sweet Freddie – he died of complications from drug abuse. Kim and Alice both died from drugs. Missy died in a DUI accident. Most of the rest, Joey, Sandy, Sharon, Nikki, Jim, and so on, went on to live lives of college, family, careers in the factories of Detroit, or being productive on some other corporate path.

I'm not sure, but if you put any group of friends at a reunion, anywhere in America, the outcome of their lives likely would not be much different, whether their zip code was 48161 in the sixties, 90210 in the eighties, or 10001 in the new century. Kids are kids, people are people, and every group's life story bears remarkable similarities.

My life has been one full of travel and adventure. Forever, the good and the bad beneath the glorious bubblegum sun will always be a part of me. It was a time that existed before technology, before Facebook, LinkedIn and Netflix – a time hidden in little towns and communities all over the country, a time when we could be, and were, the wonderful, glorious "feral" children of the 1960s.

"Turn on, tune in, drop out . . ."
~ Timothy Leary

ACKNOWLEDGEMENTS

The catalyst for Bubblegum Sun was our desire to capture the essence of adolescence and coming of age in small towns and tiny communities during the 1960s, which was inspired by true events of the decade. We drew the setting of this fictional story from our hometown of Monroe, Michigan and smaller nearby communities that rest on shores of the Great Lakes.

Places like this existed around America and almost everywhere worldwide. It is our desire that for some of our readers, this book may have taken you back to a time and perhaps a place you long to relive. For others, we hope it served as a glimpse into the past.

We would like to thank all of the people who inspired us both, now two generations of writers. We would also like to extend our thanks to our chief editor, David E. Siar, Esq., and our entire editing team for their insight and attention to detail while bringing this book to you, our readers.

Made in United States
Orlando, FL
08 January 2024

42162146R00139